A Bridge to Angels

David Traynor was born in 1966 in Merseyside and grew up in the St. Helens area. His ambition was to be a hairdresser and after attending college he qualified and with financial help from his parents opened his first salon.

As a result of his hard work and a dedicated family and staff, including his wife Andrea, he later opened a further two shops and attracted a growing list of regular clients. Later, he re-organised his business into new premises. His life seemed mapped out and settled.

After being told he had the gift of Mediumship, David began to attend development circles and has continued, with the aid of his Spirit Guides, to expand his range of skills. More recently he was informed that in the coming months he would be working to re-unite children, in the Spirit World, with their grieving parents in this, so David felt it necessary to bring together this truly moving book. Furthermore, in 2007, he was helped to develop the ability to become a physical Medium which enables him to bring Spirit Children forward to touch their parents, thus giving tangible proof that their departed children live on in the Afterlife. It has proved to be a magical, emotional experience not just for the parents but for those privileged enough to have witnessed these rare moments.

David Traynor gives regular public demonstrations of his remarkable gifts as a medium. He helps many people with their problems including grief. Each of his demonstrations is increasingly attended by a larger following of those seeking help and reassurance and requests are coming in regularly for him to travel further afield than his North-west fastness. In response to that call he will travel to New York, Scotland and the Midlands in 2008.

Previous publication: *Friends in High Places*. Published by Jade Publishing Limited, 2005.

A BRIDGE
TO ANGELS

Love & Best Wishes

David Traynor xx

David Traynor

◆JADE◆

Jade Publishing Limited,

5 Leefields Close, Uppermill, Saddleworth, Lancashire, OL3 6LA
This first impression published by Jade Publishing Limited 2008

© D. Traynor 2008
   All rights reserved worldwide

ISBN 9781900734387 A Bridge to Angels

Printed in Great Britain

Typeset by Jade Publishing Limited, Saddleworth, Lancashire, OL3 6LA

British Library Cataloguing in Publication Data
Traynor, David
A Bridge to Angels
1. Channeling (Spiritualism)
I. Title
133.9'1'092
ISBN–13: 9781900734387
Category: Mind, Body and Spirit

email: bridge@jadepublishing.com
email: davidtraynor@jadepublishing.com

www.jadepublishing.com

Contents

Acknowledgements

I would like to thank everyone, both in this life and the Afterlife, for their kind participation and for allowing us to put into print their personal stories.

Also my gratitude goes to Andrea, my lovely wife, and to Barry, my closest friend here on the Earth plane, who have supported me immensely in my work and, of course, Brian, my publisher, for his support throughout. Finally, my special thanks go to Jason, my guide, and the team on the Other Side who make all this possible.

My sincere thanks to Pamela Daniels, Jon Hoyle and Glyn Davies for their expertise in editing this, my second book; and to my Sysop, whoever he may be, for looking after my website so expertly.

God bless you all.

David Traynor
January, 2008

Illustrations

Cover by Baxter-Cox Design

Cover picture by Gareth Fielding

Dedication

To my mother Jean
in her 80th year.
I know *I'm* no angel –
so thanks for putting up with me.

Love David,
X

Preface

This afternoon, I received a most pleasant and surprising phone call. Brian called me on behalf of David Traynor and asked if I and my husband would write a few words on our experiences with David as a foreword for his new book. Of course, I was honoured, so here is my story.

I first became interested in spiritualism at an early age. When I was four years old, I recounted to my mother a conversation I had had with my great-grandmother. I can recall perfectly how she looked; down to her hair-style and even the lion's head she had on top of her walking stick. All this was as real as anything to me. My great-grandmother died two years before I was born. At the time that this was all explained to me, I was in my early teens and an avid reader. In my local library, I came across some Doris Stokes' books, borrowed them, read them and became enthralled. I went to some Spiritualist churches during my late teens, but after a few bad experiences with 'mediums', I decided it was all a hoax.

In 2001, whilst living in Spain, I got married and shortly after we fell pregnant. Unfortunately, we lost the baby at 22 weeks and I had to endure an induced labour in a foreign hospital. Nobody told us the sex of our baby, but I knew it was a boy and privately named him Callum. This hit both me and my husband hard and we chose to deal with it by not talking about it. We carried on our married life and bore two more healthy children, a boy, now four and a girl, now two. In March 2006, we started hearing noises in our house; knocking and tapping. The television would turn itself on and off, and my children started seeing a little boy in their room.

One evening, in late March, whilst reading the local paper, I saw an advertisement for 'An evening of Clairvoyance with David Traynor'. I had, two months previously, been to see another medium with my mother, but again, didn't think much of his abilities. My sister also saw the advert and mentioned it the next time we spoke. We decided to go 'as a bit of laugh' and I booked two tickets to see David.

Little did I know that night was going to change my views of mediums forever.

My sister and I saw David for the first time in April, 2006. We were lucky enough to receive a message from our grandmother who had passed about eight years previously. David described members of our family perfectly, even down to how and when they had passed. A few names and descriptions had to be clarified with other members of the family first – but they were correct. Then David surprised me by telling me there was a little boy of six or seven waiting patiently – it was he who had been making the noises etc., in our house. I could accept him. Immediately, I knew it was Callum. Sure enough, David told me that my loved ones who had passed had 'christened' him Callum. This was significant in two ways. One, because we were debating at the time whether to get my daughter christened and two, because David had got Callum's name correct. My sister and I were in awe. How could this man know something I had not told a living soul, not even my husband?! We left the meeting with tears in our eyes, but plenty of love in our hearts. My sister and I could not stop re-living the experience and vowed to see David again.

My mother and I saw David about two or three months later. Unfortunately, we weren't lucky enough to receive a reading again. Maybe because we turned up late, or moved seats during the interval, I don't know.

I was still convinced of David's ability and begged my husband to come along to David's next evening. That date is firmly etched into our memories: 9 October, 2007 – it was the day our lives changed. My husband was running late, as usual, and I advised Brian, on the door, that a 6'4" big, blond bloke would be arriving shortly and to keep a ticket for him. I paid for our tickets and took a place at the back of the room, so not to disturb anyone. My husband arrived shortly after and we settled down to enjoy the evening.

David wowed the audience again with his skill and gave positive readings to various people. Just before the interval, David pointed to us and advised us that a little boy had come through and wanted to speak to us. My husband's gasp could be heard all around the extremely quiet room. Everyone seemed to hold their breath whilst we answered, 'Yes!' David said that Callum was saying, 'Hello Mum and Dad, it's nice to be able to talk to you'. My husband and I had tears streaming down our faces, and I nearly broke my husband's hand by squeezing it so hard! David asked us if we minded if Callum touched us. You could hear a pin drop in the room, whilst I glanced at my husband to see his reaction. A slight nod, confirmed from him that he was okay with it, so I managed to squeak out a yes. David advised us we may feel a cool breeze and not to worry. Sure enough, a few moments later, we both felt a cool breeze across our right cheeks, almost as if someone was stroking them. It was the most amazing experience, better than we could ever imagine. We will never forget it. We are now content in the knowledge that our little boy is being looked after safely and will be waiting for us when it's our time to go.

During the interval, I stationed myself at the bar and drank and drank. I was in shock. My husband just kept quiet. After the show, I purposely took my time getting out of my chair and making my way to the door. I wanted to able to thank David privately without making a fool of myself in front of everyone. I did manage to talk with David and thanked him. I still thank him now from the bottom of heart. Thank you, David.

My husband is now a believer and even though David made us cry, he's still the best thing since sliced bread!

I hope you will enjoy this book and that David manages to affect you in the same way he has affected us.

Jane and Paul Potter: 'believers'.

Postscript.

I had been particularly struck by Jane and her husband that night at Bury because I remembered Jane as she came to the desk, for she had been before. She was always quiet and polite. This time we had a chat about her husband arriving late and she went through into the room. Andrea and I sat at the back, during the demonstration, about four rows behind Jane and her husband. The atmosphere was electric and the tension palpable when David asked Jane if she and her husband would like to be touched by their little boy in the Afterworld. People seated at the front all turned round to see what was to happen.

Afterwards, David and I were sitting at the desk outside the room, as usual, so people could ask David questions or buy a book. I noticed Jane standing by the doorway but keeping back, listening to others talking to David. Her husband, stood to one side away from her and he still looked stunned by the message given an hour before. When a party of about seven girls were the last to move away from the table Jane began to speak in a very clear, assured voice and addressed the 14 or so people still there. It struck me as such a remarkable and brave thing to do. The quiet, unassuming young lady I had seen on only about three occasions before had become a confident, strong and clear-speaking orator addressing a small group of strangers. This is something that most people would shy away from. Having asked Jane to write this Preface, I felt it needed her speech to be recorded for posterity but, having only vague recollections of it almost four months later, I put the question to David. He, in turn, asked Jason, his guide, so sitting in the conservatory I took notes while Jason dictated it to me through David. Marvellous.

People asked her how it felt to be touched by her child. Jane overheard someone saying how accurate David was and then heard a woman expressing her views to David that she had been a non-believer until seeing David. However, she only caught the words "non-believer" and, because of the physical experience Jane had just had and what she had witnessed on other occasions when she had watched David work, she was annoyed. Unfortunately, she had misunderstood the situation and decided to stand up for David – there and then. Her heartfelt belief is that David is genuine in what he does and she wanted to put her point of view. Here is her statement:

'After tonight who could doubt that there is life after death? Who? There was no-one more sceptical than you she said, pointing to her husband. He was a real non-believer he was. He thought it was a load old rubbish, "Didn't you?"

"Yes, I did."

"But, you don't now do you?"

"No, I don't."

I couldn't believe it – my child touched me. I felt him touch me. I couldn't believe it.'

At this stage, I think all 14 of us listening were on the brink of tears again, so passionate and strong was Jane's emotionally-charged declaration. Turning towards her husband again, Jane continued her statement ...

'All the message was correct. What he said to you was correct, wasn't it?'

"Yes," he replied.

'To make that happen, to be part of what has just happened, well, I can't believe it,' she said.

'Anyone who says it is not real – it doesn't exist – anyone who says David is false and cannot do this, doesn't know what they are saying. I came before, I've been with my mother and he was amazing then – but tonight really put the top hat on it for me and for you didn't it? Her husband simply replied, "Yes."

'If you don't believe in what he has just done, well, I don't know how you can't. It's amazing, isn't it? He just let my son come forward and touch me – my unborn child touched me! He's amazing – he's just amazing! It blows your mind!

'Sorry, sorry, I didn't mean to be rude or butt in, but I couldn't believe ... I just couldn't. We waited ages for that message and it was amazing!'

Jane's husband had become emotional because their child had stood between them and they could feel the child as he placed his hands first on their legs and then on their cheeks [though not at the same time].

I recommend you compare Jane's words and experience with that of Paula Swinnerton in a later chapter. I think you will feel the raw emotion, joy and truth that comes from their own words.

What parent would not want to make physical contact with their lost child? Can there be more tangible proof that there is an Afterlife?

Brian.

Chapter 1

Changes to come

9-35am. I was late for work – again. Wednesdays soon come around these days. Josie sat talking to Anne, waiting patiently as usual. I was still ten minutes from my hairdressing salon. I began to panic and decided to make a call from my mobile. Cheryl answered. I explained that I had overslept. Cheryl's got a great sense of humour and began to laugh and in a loud voice she shouted over to Josie and Anne:

'David's stuck behind a tractor again, he'll be here in a moment, is that O.K. ladies?' All I could hear was roars of laughter in the background.

'It's okay,' Cheryl answered. I'd been saved again. Josie's very, very patient. I'm sure her influence has rubbed off onto Anne whose patience has grown.

9-45am and I arrived at the salon. Bursting through the door, I was about to offer my apologies when Josie interrupted:

'David, these tractors are playing havoc with my Wednesday appointments! I'll have to write to my M.P., get them taken off the road, that's what I need to do.'

Everyone began to laugh. All my clients have a good sense of humour, especially the early ones. They need it with me as I'm always late.

Sue appeared from the staff room door, holding a mug of hot coffee.

'Hiya, David – stuck behind a tractor again then?'

Then, all in the same breath, without pausing, she exclaimed:

'You look tired, have you been up all night?' Silence fell over the room.

'You *do* look tired,' Josie agreed.

'He does,' Anne chipped in.

'You've been doing too much of that psycho-stuff again, it frazzles your brain that does, frazzles your brain inside your skull,' Sue declared.

Sue has a sort of down-to-earth way of expressing herself. Her personality is a cross between the characters of Peggy of *Hi-De-Hi!* and that of Vera Duckworth of *Coronation Street.* It's tinged with a little bit of Alice out of *The Vicar of Dibley* – but I'm sure you get the picture. Just as Sue finished speaking and handing me my coffee I noticed her front tooth was missing. She just reminded me so much of a serving wench, that I drawled in a pseudo-Somerset accent, ...

'... Mine's a pint of mead, wench!'

Everyone burst out laughing again, to which Sue, sticking her chest out, retorted, 'All right, Mister, I'll get it right now.' She gave a little wiggle of her hips and went back into the staff room.

Moments like that are priceless, as well as having the virtue of getting me out of a sticky question-and-answer situation – or so I thought.

Josie's hair had been washed. After applying the necessary styling products I began to blow it dry.

'Now David, you *do* look tired. I've never seen you look this way before. What's the matter, have you been up all night? Didn't you have much sleep?'

It was difficult for me to answer Josie. There were reasons, but I didn't want to go into them at that moment, so I opted for the easy way out:

'It's just been a busy week, Josie,' I replied. 'I've been helping to deliver papers for Barry from the newsagent's every Sunday morning, with 5 o'clock starts – well, they just catch up on you, you know what I mean?'

In 2005, we had to look for new business premises to relocate our salon. With the help of the Spirit World and, in particular, my Spirit Guide Jason, the premises were found just around the corner, but they incorporated a newsagent's business. So guess what? Barry, using the skills and expertise he learned during his time in the building trade, moved from hairdresser to Project Manager and began the refitting of the premises. At the same time, he ran the newsagency too. As if we hadn't enough on our plate! Well, I suppose it keeps our feet firmly on the ground. Certainly, Josie understood the commitment needed, as she had her own newsagency some years ago.

However, there were very different reasons why I had looked tired that morning. It had all started the Thursday before. I had gone to the Purple Light Spiritualist Church at Chorley as usual. It is a church I regard as being *my* church, the one I attend as often as I can. I had arrived ten minutes late – old habits die hard. The service had already started and the congregation was standing, singing one of my favourite songs; *Make me a Channel of your Peace*. I spotted a vacant chair on the second row from the back and joined in the chorus. After the song had finished everyone was asked to be seated and the Medium, who was that evening's speaker, stood up.

She was a lady I'd never seen before; rather plump with grey, curly hair and wearing glasses. Clutching a handkerchief she began rather nervously to address the congregation. It is usual in Spiritualist services for the Medium to offer a life philosophy and then give a demonstration of his or her clairvoyance, providing evidence and proof of survival after death.

This Medium began to talk about her daughter-in-law, who had longed to become pregnant, trying for many years; before ultimately being successful. She and her husband had been overjoyed; five months into her pregnancy, they had both begun to prepare their home for a new addition, decorating the spare room and buying furniture. At six months, the Medium's daughter-in-law felt that things weren't quite right. She was referred to the hospital for tests, sadly to learn that the baby had died. I could see that the Medium was deeply affected as she related the story, which was so painful for her and her family. Her daughter-in-law had given birth to a daughter, a Little Angel who hadn't quite made it here to the Earth. Understandably, she had found it very difficult to come to terms with the loss of her longed-for child. I think I can speak for all of us: the loss of a child is the greatest loss of all.

The Medium went on to explain that at Christmas she invited her family to her home for the traditional meal, as she did every year. After dining, she and her daughter-in-law were loading the dishwasher in the kitchen. The younger woman had begun to reflect on the loss of her little girl and for a moment there was silence. Then the Medium began to give a Spirit Message to her daughter-in-law. When the Spirit World chooses to give evidence of life after death without a Medium having meditated beforehand, we call this "involuntary clairvoyance". I believe it's the Spirit World saying there is a strong, immediate need for evidence. The Medium was able to provide names of members of her daughter-in-law's family and to describe past events – which she could not have known about in the normal way. Then, the daughter-in-law's grandmother came through and the Medium was able to provide evidence that the little girl, Rachael, was with her. Her grandmother kept repeating the word "Robin", but it meant little to the Medium's daughter-in-law, except as a reference to the season of the year. Later that afternoon as the family was sitting in the living room chatting, there was what could only be described as a loud tap on the window. The Medium assumed it was her next-door neighbour, whose habit it was to rap on the window, before coming into the house. The Medium asked her daughter-in-law to answer the front door and let her friend in. To her astonishment, when she opened the door there was no-one there, only a robin, comfortably perched on the Christmas tree outside, staring at her.

'Oh my God!' the daughter-in-law exclaimed.

Everyone in the living room came to the front door, thinking something was wrong. They all stared at the robin which showed no fear of so many human beings and did not move from its perch. From that moment, her daughter-in-law began to get stronger and stronger, believing in her heart that her Little Angel was safe with her grandmother in the Afterworld.

The Medium concluded her talk by saying:

'We all refer to little Rachael now as "Robin"; that's her pet name. It gives us a lot of comfort'.

I looked around the church. There wasn't a dry eye. It was a very moving testimony, so typical of many people's heartache and suffering after the loss of a child.

On the seat next to me sat a lady, aged about 70, who was thin with grey, wavy hair. She wore a three-quarter-length grey mackintosh. A man in his 40s sat next to her. He was of average build and his dark hair was thinning on top. Throughout the Medium's testimony the lady dabbed her eyes with a tissue and at one point the man put his arm around the woman's shoulder. The grief she was feeling was obviously immense. It came as no surprise to me when the Medium looked straight in our direction and with a clear gesture said:

'Can I come to you, love? You, in the grey mac?'
The lady said softly, 'Yes'.

'I've a young man here, only early 40s – maybe 41 or 42 years old, he tells me he is your son. Is this correct, my dear?'

'Yes,' was the tearful reply.

'He says "Gary", "Gary", so I'm sure this is his name, or it should mean something to you my love,' the Medium went on.

The man at the side of her piped up, 'I'm Gary'.

'This is your brother then,' the Medium asserted.

'Yes, that's correct,' he acknowledged.

'He tells me that he had problems with his head before he left this life. Do you understand?'

'I do,' Gary replied.

'I feel a tumour. Certainly a lot of problems involving my eyesight too. Do you understand this; is this correct Gary?'

'Yes, it is correct,' Gary confirmed again.

'Now he says he's better – better than when he was here. He's out of pain. Oh, there were problems in a relationship before he crossed, a separation or a divorce he's trying to show me. Is this correct?'

Gary nodded affirmatively.

I continued to look at his mother who dabbed her tears at each piece of evidence the Medium gave.

'He wants everyone to know he's sorry for all the heartache he caused before his illness. He says he was at fault. He wants you all to know this. He needs you to know he loves you all very much. It is important that you tell Linda that he does love her.'

These words had hardly left the Medium's lips when the mother gasped aloud and again began to cry.

'We will,' Gary replied, 'We'll tell Linda.'

'Now he's showing me two children, two boys around the ages of eight and eleven. I believe they are here to the Earth, so they are alive.'

'Yes,' Gary agreed.

The lady beside him said softly, 'My grandchildren.'

'I have a John now representing himself. A tall man, no hair on the top of his head; he tells me he had heart problems and crossed after a stroke. I feel that John is a father-figure. Do you understand, please?'

'Yes,' said Gary again.

'Now he's kissed your brother's head, so I know he must be very close to you. John's been on the other side for maybe five years, I think it's five years; though I'm a little confused with the way he makes me feel about that,' the Medium said. 'Is this correct?'

'No,' Gary went on, 'longer – seven years,' he corrected.

'Oh, how odd,' was the Medium's reply, 'he says five years'.

'It's five years between his crossing and my son's crossing,' the lady explained.

The Medium seemed to be content with this explanation – though not everyone in the Afterlife has a sound knowledge of how long they've been there. Here on Earth we have day and night giving us an acknowledgement of time, or the watch with which to measure time. On the other side there's only light, a sense of continual day, so no seasons or passing of the year, thus some of our loved ones can become confused when trying to judge time. We have other time markers in our world such as calendars, Bank Holidays and school terms but, nonetheless, as days run on we too sometimes lose track of time.

Finally the Medium said, 'There are two Johns, here in the Afterworld.'

'Correct,' Gary confirmed.

'I want to say your brother is also called John.'

'Yes,' Gary replied.

'Now your brother must step back. Can I leave your son's love and your brother's love with you both please?'

'Thank you,' mother and son said together.

The Medium smiled. I was impressed. No one could deny that the lady in the grey mac and her son, Gary, had received excellent communication from their loved ones in the Afterlife.

Now going back to the reason why I was tired. It was because of the following events. The Medium looked over to me.

'Can I come to you, love, you in the blue sweatshirt?'

'Yes,' I said in a loud voice, 'thanks.' A bit too loud actually. I felt a bit foolish. It made a few people in the congregation laugh, including the Medium.

'Now my love, as I stand in front of you, I am told by my inspirers that you also are a Medium and that the Spirit World works with you a lot. Is this correct?'

'Yes,' I replied, curious as to what she was going to say next.

'They tell me you work well with people. They feel at ease with you and I'm told you're going to be working with children.'

'Children?' I said, somewhat incredulously.

'Yes, children; people's Little Angels in the Spirit World. I'm told this will be relevant. Can you watch out when you're joined by children in the Afterworld, love?'

'Children?' I queried a second time.

'Don't look so astonished,' she went on, 'when children in the Spirit World have enough trust to work with you, it's because – well, it's because you are trustworthy. You must be a good person. Children there know who they like and who they dislike, in the same way as they do on the Earth plane. My mother had a saying: "Children always know who's good to them," so don't be shocked, love, be flattered.'

'Thanks,' I replied, still feeling bemused by the information.

I remembered reading a Doris Stokes book (she was a Medium, who often saw and worked with children in the Afterlife). I thought to myself, 'Well, if it's good enough for the most famous Medium ever known, it's good enough for me, the best-known unknown.'

'Many parents are going to be seeking you out because they want to contact their children in the Spirit World. You'll be like a bridge, love. I'm seeing a bridge and you'll be going backwards and forwards over it – a Bridge to Angels. Spirit Children will make themselves known to you. Welcome them with open arms. Where they are, there is only love. Now with that I'm going to leave you and say, "Good luck, my dear".'

In a split second, she had moved on to a gentleman near the front of the congregation.

I was shocked to say the least – the very least. Even though I do this work, it never ceases to amaze me. It always leaves me with countless questions that I'd like to ask – O.K., I exaggerate, but certainly a great many questions. Absolutely enthralled by what she had said, I sat with my eyes fixed on the Medium, hanging on her every word. As she was coming to the end of the demon-stration, I noticed a little girl had stepped forward from the Afterworld. She stood at the side of the Medium. She was about seven or eight years old, with long, curly hair. I could see her plainly, as if she were in the land of the living, smiling coyly at the Medium, who did not look at her or acknowledge her presence at all. Then I saw the little girl point out a lady on the end of the front row. The Medium, meanwhile, thanked her last communicator and then gestured towards the lady the child had indicated.

'Can I come to you, love?'

'Yes,' the lady nodded.

The Medium went on to describe the little girl perfectly – giving her age, what she was wearing, in fact every detail. However, she still didn't acknowledge the little girl, as far as I could tell. The lady wept openly. Every scrap of evidence, every detail the

Medium gave, the lady acknowledged as being correct. After she had given the message, the little girl waved and walked away into the ether. The Medium thanked us all for being a good congregation and sat down. We all gave her a round of applause, she deserved it.

That night when I returned home, Andrea, my wife, was on the couch watching TV; Barry, my best mate who lives with us, had gone to bed as he has to get up early to sort and deliver the papers at our newsagency.

'There are some emails for you.' Andrea pointed to a small pile of print-outs on the unit.

'Would you like a hot drink, love?' she asked.

'Please,' I replied, kicking off my shoes.

I began to read the emails. The first one began:

'Hi, my name is Anne. We lost our child two years ago. We were wondering if you could help us.'

The second email asked:

'Hello, David. We saw you at Liverpool SNU Church the other night. We lost our son, who was five years old, three years ago. Can you help?'

The third email:

'Hi there, I have had a miscarriage, David. I'm in a desperate, desperate situation. I need to know my child lives on. Can you help me?'

Talk about forcing your arm up your back! Another one read:

'Hi, I lost my daughter Michelle with breast cancer three years ago. Can you contact her for me please? I need to know she's okay.'

This was no ordinary coincidence. Anyone who knows and understands the Spirit World will tell you that this type of organisation by Spirit happens all the time. What was strange was that all the emails were about contacting people's children. They had also given me half of the information, half of the evidence, which is really unnecessary and unwelcome. If you seek communication with a loved one in the Afterworld, it's best just to say to the Medium: 'We want you to communicate for us'. The Medium should be able to give you knowledge about the loved one. You should understand, also, that we Mediums are able to work better if the information we are given is kept to the minimum. Thus, we may be assured that the evidence we receive *is* from the Spirit World and not our own imagination creating situations around what we already know.

Those who grow in spiritual wisdom come to realise the difference. The less information the public gives a Medium, the better. As I always say to those who consult me, 'If *I* tell *you*, you are more likely to believe that the messages I pass on from the Spirit World are really and truly coming from your loved ones.' I suppose that's why it's difficult to "read" for your own friends and family, simply because you already know so much about them.

Chapter 2

Little Visitors

However, to return to the night I came back from the Purple Light Spiritualist Church. Andrea had a 'flu virus, which had hung around all week, so she sat hunched over her cup of hot chocolate. Poor girl, there was more life in a soluble Aspirin! And me? Well, I'd demonstrated Mediumship every night that week. I'd have passed for one of Madame Tussaud's wax dummies. We were a sad and sorry sight as we sat there staring at a re-run of an episode of the television comedy *Only Fools and Horses*. I just couldn't help thinking to myself how apt the title was – fools working like horses.

When we retired to bed, Andrea was out like a light but, strangely, I must have caught an unwelcome second wind, which caused me to stay awake. I lay on my back, wide-eyed, watching the atmosphere dancing around me. The room was alive with energy moving from one corner of the room to another. It went from the dressing table to the doors of our *en suite* bathroom, where the energy pattern changed to stripes – a bit like the patterns you see if your TV set isn't tuned in properly. I couldn't take my eyes off it. I'm never, ever frightened, but once my curiosity is ignited – well, I can forget sleep.

This display of energy, this sort of dance went on for what seemed ages and eventually my mind and body must have given in and I fell asleep. During the early hours, I could hear a voice faintly calling my name: 'David! David!', repeatedly. I opened my eyes to see a little boy looking at me. He seemed so real that I jerked my head back, banging it on the headboard. Andrea slept on. The boy appeared to be about five years old. He had thick, curly, mousy-brown hair and big brown eyes. He was a beautiful child with a radiant smile. Instinctively, I knew that he was a Spirit Child. As I looked at him, my thoughts began to gather. The boy said nothing, but he smiled at me. Speaking through thoughts so as not to disturb Andrea, I began to communicate with him.

'Hello. What's your name?' I said in my "head" voice. (For those of you who haven't read my first book *Friends in High Places*, my head voice is that which I use when I read to myself – just as you are probably doing at this moment).

'Stephen.'

'And why are you here?'

'To get sweets and lollipops and to play with my friends.'

'Where's your money?' I enquired.

He just smiled.

'You don't want to buy sweets and lollipops from me then, Stephen?'

'No. I want you to give me them,' he answered, grinning.

'Have you got a mummy? Is your mummy with you?'

He just carried on smiling for a moment then began to wander around the bedroom. As he did, the atmosphere around him was slightly illuminated; again, almost alive, buzzing. Then, next to him, I could see a little girl, perhaps slightly younger, with blonde, wavy hair, who was wearing a little blue and white dress, which just reminded me of a tablecloth my great aunt used to have. The girl was laughing and jumping up and down in my bedroom.

'Hello,' I said to her, again using my head voice.

'Hello,' she giggled back.

'Who are *you* then? Do you have a name?' I asked.

'Yes ... guess,' she suddenly said.

'O.K. – Susan?'

'No.'

'Amy?'

'No,' she giggled, again.

'Charlotte?'

'No.'

'Michelle?'

'No.'

'Rosie?'

'No,' she chuckled with glee.

After reaming off what seemed to be every female name in the book, I said in a last ditch attempt, 'Elizabeth.'

They both pealed with laughter and with a strong gesture, quite out of the ordinary for so small a child, she replied animatedly, 'You've got it!' and she struck a pose a little like a dancer at the end of a performance. Then something totally unexpected happened: a huge white-faced owl appeared perching on a ledge outside the bay window of our bedroom. I have seen it many times; I think it's a barn owl. There are many owls where I live and lots of other wildlife. In many parts of Britain the expansion of man has led to the destruction of the habitats of many animals, birds and plants, so I feel very privileged to live where I do and to enjoy their presence. The reason I could see the owl so clearly from our bed, was because we had ordered new curtains which had not yet arrived. The owl, in its turn, could clearly see me through the window and it remained on its perch staring fixedly at me. But I had the distinct impression that it was there for a purpose. It gave a prolonged, loud screech and the children were no longer in the room. Was it in some way connected with them? Had it appeared when it did to stop them bothering me?

I glanced at my watch, which showed 5-20. I must have been awake all night, or so it seemed. I realised suddenly that I had not heard Barry leave and that he had overslept by about an hour. Leaping out of bed and rushing to his room, I shouted 'Barry! Get up! You've overslept!'

In my anxiety, I glanced at his digital alarm clock. It said 1-15, but I didn't take in the relevance of this at first. 'Come on, Barry!'

'What?' Barry exclaimed with annoyance.

I looked over at the clock again: 1-16. Slowly, I began to realise that it was only 1-16 in the morning. I checked my watch, which still said 5-20. It had stopped. Yet, at midnight, just before I went to bed, I was sure my watch confirmed the end of the day. Now it's things like that that really "spook" *me*. Creeping back out of Barry's room, I looked at my watch again. I decided to put it on the window-sill. Andrea was still in bed, out for the count. I slipped in beside her to try to get some sleep. No chance. My mind was so active. I even tried some simple meditations but soon gave up.

Eventually, I could hear the dawn chorus. By this time I was irritated, sombre and tetchy. If I had had a gun handy, there would have been no choir of birds tweeting in the sunrise – just me in my blue-spotted boxers and white T-shirt, two dark circles around my eyes, surrounded by feathers.

Chapter 3

A start at St Helens

During the course of the morning I began to have twinges of toothache. I'd had a little warning sign previously but, because I don't like dentists that much, I put my need for a filling on hold. May I hasten to add that I like the dentist as a person, but it seems to me that he changes personality when he gets a pair of forceps or a syringe in his hand. You lie back with your mouth open wide, there's a tube sucking out your saliva, then you have the dentist probing into your mouth. Once the problem has been identified a syringe may be needed to administer the anaesthetic. Next, perhaps, comes the placing of a long piece of cotton wool down the side of your gum – a bit like a draught-excluder – and, just as your nerves are at breaking point, he calmly asks you: 'All right then, are you going on any holidays this year?' And for some strange reason, after three grunts from me, he knows I'm off to Lanzarote for a week!

Anyway, I'm going off my tale. I rang the dentist's and his receptionist managed to fit me in at 3pm, which I appreciated. The allotted time soon came round and I found myself sitting in his waiting area where I picked up a copy of the popular magazine *Hello!* to while away the time. The receptionist sat staring into space. Opposite her was a man in his early 70s, dressed in black trousers, blue shirt and a grey mac. He leaned back, holding onto his walking stick, obviously waiting for his turn. After a period of total silence, the receptionist blurted out:

'What do you think about these Psychics and Mediums, Mr Roberts? Do you believe they can do what they say? You know what I mean – do you believe they can talk to our relatives who are dead? Or do you think it's all rubbish then?'

I couldn't believe my ears. Several things ran through my mind: 1) Was she aware that I am a Medium and wanted me to join in the conversation so that, perhaps, I would be able to tell her something she wanted to know; 2) was she genuinely interested; or 3) was she a bit of a maniac who hated Mediums and was going to pull a gun out from her desk drawer to shoot me? I didn't care, because my tooth was aching so much I just needed to be put out of my misery.

I could tell that Mr Roberts was a gentleman and with much sincerity he replied:

'Well, I've always believed it *can* be done, but I do not think we should try to communicate with the dead. My mother always said that when you invite that type of energy or force into your life, that's when your problems start and everything begins to go wrong. It's a force you don't need. You're better leaving the people in the other world alone. That's what I believe.'

Mr Roberts paused briefly and then added:

'I've lost my son and my wife, but I know they're around me all the time. I don't need to be told. That's my view for what it's worth.'

I sank low behind my magazine. Then Mr Roberts was summoned into the surgery and, simultaneously, the phone rang and the receptionist began to speak, 'Oh hi, you all right? I've just been talking to one of our clients – you must be psychic!' She began to laugh. 'What time does it start then? Eight o'clock. O.K. Meet you at seven on the car park; we can go for a drink first. O.K. Oh yes, I've heard he's very good. What's his name again? David Traynor. No, I just couldn't remember it, that's all.'

I sank lower into my chair thinking that she must be coming to see me at the Hilton Hotel, St Helens tonight. She can't have realised it's me. She put the phone down.

'David Traynor – would you like to come through please?' said a female voice.

As calm as jelly I put down my magazine and walked into the surgery. The receptionist gave no sign of having connected this David Traynor with the name she had uttered 20 seconds before. The dentist gave me the news that my tooth had had it and would have to come out. Shell-shocked, I agreed to stay and have it removed. I just hoped the pain and the anaesthetic would have worn off by the time I reached The Hilton that evening. 'I should be so lucky,' I thought.

I was given an injection to numb my gum and sent out into the waiting area whilst the anaesthetic took effect. Minutes later, when I returned, my gum hadn't become numb. Six needles later, my gum began to go dead and finally at 4-30pm, the tooth which had caused me all the pain had been removed. I reported to the reception desk to pay my dues.

She obviously still made no connection between the David Traynor of the phone call and the David Traynor standing before her. Politely, I paid up and left. As I exited from the surgery, I saw Mr Roberts talking to a gentleman on the pavement outside. I couldn't help thinking about the answer he had given the dental receptionist and I didn't realise then how much his answer would plague me in the coming months. The bleeding caused by the extracted tooth stopped within minutes but I couldn't feel my tongue, my ear, my neck nor, strangely enough, the edge of my nose.

By 6-30pm I had begun to panic. 'Why?' you may ask. Well, a spirit uses the body of a Spirit Medium in so many ways, to bring messages across for the audience member or the sitter. For instance, they can transmit physical feelings to the body of the Medium to help him or her understand how they left our world. They can heighten the Medium's sense of awareness in different parts of the body, such as the stomach. They do not transmit pain, but the sensations suggest it. Then they can implant the single word "cancer" in the Medium's mind. He or she will then realise that the Spirit means stomach cancer. It is obviously important for the Medium to be in a position to accept these feelings. If, at 6-30pm, he has a sore mouth, swollen face, a partially anaesthetised head and he has a demonstration at 8pm, the Medium will panic. And I did!

I reached The Hilton at 7-15. The sound equipment had arrived and was set up. Everything looked great. People were beginning to arrive. The foyer was almost full. A lovely young lady led me to the room where I would be able to prepare myself for clairvoyance.

As we approached the room I thanked her, but just as she turned round to leave, I could sense a little boy walking beside her. When I say "sense", at first it was just the sense of a little boy, but as I focused I could actually see the little boy clearly. He looked to be, maybe, three or four years old, no older. 'Excuse me!' I exclaimed, 'I just wondered if you have a little boy in the Afterlife by any chance? He's three, or maybe four and he's running around you right now.'

The girl looked shocked and pale.

'No, no! I don't,' she replied.

'How strange. He's shouting "mum, mummy" at you.'

'No,' the young lady replied very definitely. 'No – I don't know who he could be,' she added.

'Would you like me to find out?' I asked.

'Yes please, if you don't mind, just in case he's a friend's child or something ...' Her voice trailed off.

'I don't mean to frighten you, love,' I told her, 'usually, I don't say anything outside a demonstration or a sitting, because not everyone wants to know about the Spirits around them.'

'Well I do,' she insisted, 'I really want to know, so it is O.K. if you tell me.'

An older man was standing in the corner of the corridor. He was definitely in the Spirit but made no attempt to approach me.

'Hello sir, who are you?' I asked in my head voice.

'I'm James,' he replied. 'This child's my great grandchild.'

'O.K. And why are you here, James?'

'I am the young lady's grandfather.'

'Welcome.'

I repeated the name and the information to the lady.

'James is my grandfather,' she confirmed. 'Can you describe him?' she went on.

'Of course,' I replied. 'He's about 5'9", a very well-built man, a full head of white, wavy hair, gold-rimmed glasses on.'

'That's definitely my grandad,' she said, rather shocked.

'He was 76 when he passed. He's just told me. Is that correct?'

'Yes,' the girl replied.

James then begin to make the side of my head feel strange. What was particularly odd was that the side of my head, that he was making to feel peculiar, was the side which was still numb as result of the anaesthetic. On top of that, he was making my heart beat faster. All at once, the side of my face felt cold.

'Did James have a heart attack and a stroke?' I asked.

'Yes he did,' she said.

'This is what took James from this life to the next, wasn't it?'

'Sadly, yes it was,' she agreed.

'Who is the child, James?' I asked in my head voice.

'My granddaughter lost a child three years ago, a boy – Stephen.'

I thanked him.

'He says the boy's name is Stephen, a miscarriage, three years ago, at about seven weeks.'

The girl began to cry.

'Yes, David it's true. I really didn't realise. I'm sorry, I wasn't trying to confuse you or lie,' she sobbed. 'He's a boy you say?'

'Yes, he's lovely.'

'I knew, I just knew he was a boy. Is he all right? What does he look like?'

'Just like any other toddler of that age. He's got fine, brown, straight hair, chubby cheeks. He's lovely.'

'Thank you so very much, David,' she repeated.

'James tells me he and your gran, Mary, are taking care of Stephen for you.'

'You know, "Stephen" was what I would have called him if he had lived. It's one of my favourite names. I was in a violent relationship at the time and I needed to move on. I wasn't married, we just lived together. He was an awful man. I can't tell you how badly he treated me. I was glad my first child would not grow up to know him as his father. But, with the help of my family and friends, I left him.

The young lady was quite overcome with emotion. I said quietly, 'In our lives, things happen that sometimes we regret.

However, you know now that your son lives and he is here with you. Have peace in that knowledge.'

'I didn't even know they grew up in Heaven,' the girl replied.

'Oh yes. Usually, the unborn grow to the age of natural learning, which is from five to seven years of age, sometimes older. Then they may decide to be born again – reincarnated.'

The girl interjected, 'He may decide to have another shot at life?'

'Yes. He may decide to take another body. The body is only a vehicle that moves around this physical Earth.

'Oh, so he can do that?' she wanted to know.

'If he so chooses. It's a free-will universe, love.'

'David, I can't thank you enough. I just know I can begin to put the whole situation behind me and move on. Please David, has he gone?'

'No. He's still here. I can still see him with James.'

'Tell him I love him and I'm sorry he didn't make it.'

'You just did that,' I replied.

'Thanks very much.'

The girl kissed me and walked off down the corridor, followed by her little shadow.

I've always said to everyone, the Spirits have a strange way of letting you know "you'll be all right on the night" to coin a phrase. So even though I still had a numbed head, everything was going to be all right. My physical condition wasn't going to stop the Spirit people passing messages on to their loved ones. But that night, I was very conscious that although I'm only human, I should, perhaps, put more trust in the wonderful gift of clairvoyance I have been given.

The first lady I acknowledged during the demonstration that night was a rather large, attractive lady, smartly dressed, who seemed very serious, which is not uncommon at demonstrations. You could tell she was nervous. I always try to put people at their ease, because their minds and their expectations of what is going to happen may make them uncomfortable and nervous. I have a saying, which is, "I don't bite unless you ask me to!" Usually, this makes people laugh and eases the tension. As I began to talk to her, I could sense she had a great need for healing. My shirt was beginning to stick to my back as the heat poured from me across to the lady. When I looked over at her, I saw she was beginning to perspire about the head. She dabbed her forehead with a tissue.

'Are you hot, love?' I asked.

'I'm boiling, you must be hot stuff!' she joked.

The audience broke out into laughter.

'The hotter the better!' was my retort.

'You would understand there is a strong need for healing in your life at this moment, my dear,' I said.

'Yes,' the lady affirmed.

'I feel very strongly that it's needed right now. I need to say to you it is most important and this is why we are both experiencing such tremendous heat. A heated moment between us!' I joked.

'I have a lady joining me now who tells me her name is Vera but most people called her Joan. Do you understand?'

'Correct,' the lady replied.

'This lady makes me feel very motherly towards you. She wants to play mum with you. I don't know why she's making me want to mother you, but she is.'

At this point the lady became very emotional.

'She tells me there are two Veras.'

'There are,' she trembled.

'This Vera, whom people called Joan, brought you up. She's your grandmother and the other Vera, who crossed over young, is your mother. Is that right?'

'That's correct.'

'So they called her Joan because it was her second name?' I queried.

'No, that's wrong,' the lady replied.

'No?' I echoed, surprised, because that piece of information felt so correct.

'So there's something about a second name – Joan, Jones, something like that she's trying to make me say.'

'Correct,' the lady answered, 'Her second name is Jones.'

'O.K.'

I sometimes find, during a demonstration, that my own logical mind does not piece together correctly the information I'm given. I continued.

'When Vera was at school, she was called Joan and the name stuck throughout her life?' I ventured.

'That's right,' said the lady, 'when my nan was at school, there were three Veras in her class, so two of them adopted second names to avoid confusion.'

'Don't feed the Medium,' I interrupted.

'Well, I thought you were confused,' the lady said to me.

'Confused? Me? Well, it's not difficult!' I laughed.

This broke a tension in the room. Everybody began to laugh.

'I'm going to call this lady Joan now, this lady who is your nan, simply because it will be less confusing for you. Joan tells me that you need to know that both your mother and your grandmother will be with you throughout the operation. You have been worrying about this operation, but you need to know you will not be alone.'

At this point the lady wept openly. Another lady at her side instantly put her arms around her and gave her a cuddle. Clairvoyance certainly brings out the very best in people. Frequently at my demonstrations, I have witnessed complete strangers get up from their seats to hug others who have been sitting alone. This energy, this atmosphere that is created by uniting the Spiritual with the physical, brings with it a sense of caring and compassion that I have never seen elsewhere.

I continued, 'Joan takes me to open-heart surgery for some reason.'

'Yes, I have to have open heart surgery.'

'This is imminent,' I stated.

'Is tomorrow close enough?' the lady asked.

A concerted gasp broke the silence of the audience, a silence that emphasised that they had just heard the truth. Although the evidence that the Spirits provide us with is truthful, sometimes it is so detailed and accurate that people can't help but gasp.

'They're sending out their thoughts of love and kindness towards you, my love. Trust. You will not be alone. Trust in the comfort that your loved ones will guide the surgeon's hands. Trust, love, in the face of adversity, have trust.'

'Thank you, David,' the lady said quietly.

'Now your mother, Vera, is coming forward. She is quite a large lady with black, wavy, shoulder-length hair and wearing glasses with pointed frames.'

'Correct.'

'Your mum crossed when she was about 38.'

'That is correct,' she replied.

'She tells me she crossed out of life quickly.' I felt it appropriate to click my fingers. 'Out like a candle,' I said.

'Correct.'

'She collapsed and then she was gone.'

'Yes David.'

'She tells me that because of the suddenness of her crossing, you are concerned that the same will happen to you. You look like your mother, you have the same ailments as your mother and you are frightened. That is your fear, that you will cross over whilst you are still young, like her.'

'Yes David, I'm terrified. I feel I've everything to live for.'
Every part of her shook, so I realised that she was terribly frightened. Sometimes, revealing our true fears gives us a sense of absolute terror.

'You know, by tomorrow evening this nightmare will be behind you and you must then look to the future. Since your mother left the physical plane, medicine has changed dramatically. She says she was ill for a couple of years and her problem was not diagnosed correctly.'

'That's true David,' she replied.

'So what's the difference?' I asked.

The lady looked puzzled. 'I don't know,' she said slowly.

'Well, the difference is that you've been diagnosed. You have a problem and tomorrow you will have the problem corrected.'

'Goodness! I never thought of it like that. Thanks David. But you're right.'

'I'm not right love, your mother is. Although she is in the Spirit World, your mum is still your mum. She needs to comfort you. Now your mum has two girls joining her. They crossed over as babies. They're twins.'

'Oh!' the lady exclaimed. 'Yes, David, yes. My babies. Oh please, please!' she cried. 'They were premature.'

'What do "one" and "six" mean to you?'

'One lived for 24 hours, the other for six days.'

'Well, both are here now joining your mother. She tells me that as your nan took care of you in your mother's physical absence, she is taking care of your daughters in yours. Both girls are blowing kisses to you now, my love. Who is Emma, please?'

'That's my daughter who lived for six days. I'm sorry David ...' she sobbed.

'You don't have to apologise to me, my love, for being emotional. And Kirsty, who's Kirsty?'

'That's my other daughter who lived one day.'

'Look, I need to leave all their love with you for always, but just be aware that when you have your surgery tomorrow, your loved ones will all be there at your side, loving you, watching you, healing you with the love of Spirit.'

The room broke out with a huge round of applause.

'Thank you. Thank you, David. Thank you so much,' the lady repeated.

When the Spirit people come along to connect with their loved ones who are here on the Earth plane, they do so with the help of my Guides. Jason, my own Guide, makes it possible for me to connect with an audience or with one-to-one sitters. It is through Jason that I am able to link to their loved ones in Spirit. Amazing. It definitely is a spiritual bridge to our loved ones.

At the end of my demonstrations I usually take a seat near the entrance of the room or hall. Audience members come over, maybe to purchase a book, or ask a question, or pass their opinion on the evening's event. At the end of this demonstration at the Hilton Hotel, St. Helens, a young lady hurried over to me, whilst people queued behind her waiting their turn to speak.

'Hello, have you enjoyed tonight?' I asked.

'Yes, but I hoped someone would come through for me – well, us.'

As she spoke, she began to cry. The older lady standing by her side took hold of her and said, 'Come on love, cheer up.'

I reached over and took the young girl's hand. I did so to comfort her, but then I realised her brother was in the Spirit. I looked at the other lady, whom I knew to be her mother.

'My love, you have a son in the Spirit World.'

The now tearful older lady replied, 'Yes, yes I have.'

'Would he be John?'

'Oh yes,' the young girl exclaimed.

At this point, all the people who stood forming an orderly queue behind them gathered round in a rough horseshoe shape to listen in.

'Can you understand, please, that he crossed in a vehicle accident? He's showing me a motorbike.'

'Yes. Is he there?' asked his mother.

'He is, love. He's fine. He's bringing through another John.'

'My dad!' the girl exclaimed, 'That's who he is. The other John's my dad. Is he there too?' 'Is he here as we speak?' her mother wanted to know.

'Your brother John tells me you've been having a difficult time, young lady.'

As I spoke these words I squeezed her hand in rhythm with the words, so that she would focus on what I was saying.

'He tells me you've split up from your fiancé; he's hurt you.'

'Yes, yes,' she sobbed

'He's Steve, your ex.'

'No, Steve's my younger brother.'

'Oh, O.K. love,' I said, 'I can be wrong.'

I must add at this point, that all Mediums can be wrong when they are listening or picking up sensations and feelings from the Spirit World.

'Hold on. There's a connection with Rob.'

'That's him,' she replied. 'That's my ex. That's the one, that's the one who's hurt me.'

'O.K. Your brother wants you to know he's watching and cares deeply what has happened in your relationship. I want you to know he watches everything and he wants to support you. It is a difficult time for you, love. He tells me there's a house up for sale.'

'Yes, there is,' the young lady replied.

'Trust. Things will be sorted out for you. You can move on and get on with your life then.'

'Thank you, David,' she replied.

'I'll leave his love with you both.'

They both walked away obviously much affected, but I'm sure they were both pleased that they had received some communication from their loved one. The Hilton Hotel, St Helens had proved to be one of my more emotional demonstrations. My job was over.

We began to pack up the equipment when a little face popped round the door.

'Hey, David, David,' a voice whispered.

I turned around, walked over to the door and moved through it into the foyer. There stood the lovely lady who was due to have open-heart surgery the following day.

'David. You were spot-on, love. Thanks, thanks for what you said. All my fears have gone now. Thank you.'

The lady gave me a big hug and kissed me on the cheek.

'God bless you, David,' she said as she walked away.

A sense of peace came over me.

'Thanks, gang,' I said to my guides in my head voice.

'No, thank *you* David,' came back the reply.

Chapter 4

Michelle

It's a busy life being a Medium. My Mediumship takes me to different parts of the country. In addition, I take services at Spiritualist churches and I also have my private sittings; my private surgery for those who are really suffering after bereavement, or for those who are desperate for guidance in their lives.

One such sitting stands out in my mind. It came about after a young lady had been along to one of my demonstrations near Manchester. Her name is Michelle. On that night nothing had come through for her, but she'd been desperate, I mean really desperate, to hear from someone in the Afterworld. I received a phone call from my good friend Brian Prescott. He's not only a good friend, he's also my publisher, which is quite handy I suppose. Mind you, he also co-ordinates my tours, compiles the advertising schedule, prepares and supplies the advertisements to the various newspapers and is responsible for tickets and bookings. He also tells me off if I need to be told off. Gosh! Brian's more like my guardian here on Earth: a sort of surrogate father-figure standing in for my real dad who is on the other side.

Anyway, Brian called me up. 'I've had a phone call from a young lady. She sounds pretty desperate David. She came along to your event at Ashton-under-Lyne but didn't receive a message. She really is in need.'

When Brian is keen for me to help someone he sort of staccatos every word. The words which are really important, such as 'desperate', he highlights with his voice. That's probably the subconscious wordmonger coming out in him, but when Brian says it's desperate, I know it is. I'd arranged to go out for a meal at a friend's house close by in the next village the following Friday, but I decided to cancel this and rebook it a few weeks later. So, now I had a date free for "one-to-ones".

'Go on then, Brian; see if she can come then.'

Brian agreed. He put the phone down to ring Michelle to see if that would be convenient. He rang back almost immediately.

'Yes, that's fine David. Michelle sounds really happy with that suggestion.'

What Brian didn't know then was that Michelle had no transport and what I'm about to say will probably make you all understand why Brian is my right-hand man. He agreed to collect the girl and bring her across for her sitting. The man's an Angel – well, most of the time.

Friday came round. My first sitting, a lady and gentleman nearly drove me mad. They arrived at seven, both carrying black bin bags. They seemed friendly enough. They'd waited ages for a one-to-one sitting and in fact they told me they were present at one of my early demonstrations at Preston. Anyway, don't get me wrong, they seemed lovely people and both had very strong Irish accents. The lady wore glasses and had natural red hair, typical of her Celtic origin. Monica was dressed very simply and she'd kept her slippers on. Obviously, she was intent on making herself at home. James, her husband, was as bald as a coot: no hair, no eyebrows, nothing. It seemed possible to me he'd had alopecia or some related illness that makes you lose your hair. I remembered speaking to them when I was making a booking a few weeks before, but they rang again later and said they were unable to keep that appointment. So when this night had become available I decided that I would see them first and then the young lady, Michelle.

Monica, James's wife, had asked if they could bring along some personal effects to help communication. I explained that it wasn't really necessary, but she became insistent on the phone, so to save time I just agreed. Both sat on the back couch in my conservatory staring into space. Both looked emotional. I could really feel the intensity of their sorrow and grief.

'I have a gentleman joining me from the World of Spirit,' I said, confidently. 'A smallish gentleman, 5'3" maybe 5'4" tall. He has grey-white hair, combed right over to one side. He tells me that he went out from this life like a light, with a heart attack. Gives me the name of Fred. Makes me feel he's a father, a fatherly link, so he must be your father?'

I gestured towards Monica.

'Yes he was,' she replied.

But she just seemed unimpressed. She seemed to brush the information off as if it were absolutely trivial. James looked at her and then at me.

'It's not the family we want to speak to,' he chipped in.

'O.K., O.K.,' I said, 'but it's a bit difficult to do Mediumship to order, James. I can't summon up people in the Afterworld, I can only tell you who is here at this moment.'

'We understand that,' James replied. 'Here, see if you can get anything from this.'

Before I could say anything, Monica had reached into her bin bag and placed a lovely carved wooden trinket box into my hand.

'I'll try,' I replied.

It had been a long time since I had practised psychometry. This is the word we use to describe the technique of holding something physical, *eg* a watch, and using the item to connect with a loved one in the Spirit World, it helps to strengthen the link and the communication. Taking hold of the fancy box I immediately found I was listening to a phone ringing. It was so clear. When I told the couple, James exclaimed, 'I'm astonished!'

'Someone's shouting the name of Charles. "Charles" is being called out to me clearly,' I said.

Monica began to cry.

'That's my baby. Oh my Charles. That's my baby.'

With no clue whatsoever as to what was going on, I continued.

'I don't see a child right now in the Afterworld. Charles isn't representing himself. However, he must have had a pet bird. I'm seeing a mynah bird.'

I knew the breed of bird because my aunty had had one when I was a child.

'That's not to say Charles won't represent himself if we carry on,' I explained to them.

Both looked astonished.

'Can I open the box?' I asked.

'Of course,' they replied.

Carefully I undid the clasp thinking that its contents might help me to bring through their child a little stronger. As I did so, I had the shock of my life. In the box was a mynah bird. It was obvious to me that it had been to a taxidermist; it was stuffed. It lay on its side. I didn't know what to say. I didn't know whether to laugh or cry, or how to react. Perspiration flowed from my forehead but Providence prevailed.

At this point Monica said, in a matter-of-fact tone, 'Meet Charles, my baby. Say hello, Charles.'

James repeated, 'Hello, Charles.'

Best to follow suit I thought, so I said, 'Oh, hello Charles.'

At that point I can remember the thoughts coming through my head, 'I think I'm going mad, I'm now talking to a bird that has been stuffed, lying in a box. Pinch yourself David. You are going mad!'

'Great evidence!' Monica exclaimed. 'Great! He always mimicked our phone, all the time, didn't he James?'

'He did. He never stopped doing that.'

Before I knew it, on the floor of my conservatory was one rabbit called Abraham, again stuffed, one stuffed budgie called Pepper (there could be a joke in there somewhere) but it's all on the level and a lovely coloured bird called Chez – to this day I couldn't tell you what species it was, but it too was stuffed. They were all presented in boxes, all lay on their sides. The temptation to laugh was totally overcome by the anticipation of what was going to be pulled out of the bin bag next. And it wasn't anticipation unfulfilled.

Time had flown by and I was feeling the sitting had to be drawn to a conclusion, before I would be able to lay claim to being the only Spirit Medium who had housed a full zoo of dead creatures in his conservatory. I explained it was the end of the sitting. Monica smiled.

'You know, David, we never had children of our own. These lovely animals were our children weren't they James?'

'Yes they were, love. Thanks for your time, it's been very special.'

Monica loaded the boxes into the bags. Both shook my hand and I led them out.

'See you again,' I said.

After waving bye-bye to them I came back inside and sat down in the conservatory trying to regain my composure ready for the next sitting. Suddenly in my head I could hear someone speaking. I closed my eyes to focus on the voice. It said: 'Man or beast, it is always hard to let go of someone or something we love with all our heart. Man or beast, we're all children in the sight of God. Man or beast, we are all loved by someone.' The voice stopped. I felt ever so guilty. I'd done nothing wrong, but I still felt a sense of guilt so I just said out loud, 'Sorry.' I hoped my apology would be accepted for whatever I had done wrong.

As I looked up, Brian was entering the dining room, followed by a young lady in her mid-30s and a young man of about the same age. Brian introduced her and her boyfriend to me. They looked nervous. Sometimes, if you tell people they look nervous it helps them because it gives them a chance to say how they're feeling. I'm so used to talking to people in the other world that it really is nothing at all for me, but people who are not used to Spirit communication can be very nervous indeed; I have on occasions witnessed people shaking. So if you give them a chance to tell you how they are feeling about it, it usually puts them at their ease. May I add at this point, that when they are telling me how they are feeling, I make sure they don't slip into telling me who they have come to talk to or why they have come? It's fine to know their fears, but I feel to know anything more would be to compromise the purity of the messages I subsequently give.

'You look frightened, Michelle,' I said.

'I am. He is too.'

'Well don't be. You're in good company and safe hands. Are you both sitting together?' I asked.

Brian looked over to her boyfriend, Steve.

'Are you going in with Michelle? You can go in if you like.'

'No, I'll stay here. You go in,' he said quickly.

'O.K. It looks like I'm on my own then,' Michelle replied.

I left Brian in the dining room talking to Michelle's other half.

'Michelle, can I ask you to sit on the back couch please?'

She did so. Then I explained to her that I wanted her to say "yes" or "no" to my questions. "Yes" if what I said was correct and "no" if it was wrong. Nothing else. Michelle still was very nervous. She sat clutching her bag.

'I have a gentleman coming forward, Michelle. He had problems around the chest area, with his lungs, before he crossed from this life to the Afterlife. I feel he is a grandfather link to you. He gives me the name William – Bill. Do you understand, Michelle?'

'Yes,' she replied.

'Also, there is a lady coming forward, a grandmother. She was immobile before she crossed. The lady was very, very breathless. She says to me that your family was great to her before she crossed to the Spirit World.'

'This is correct,' Michelle replied.

'She's just confirmed to me she is your grandmother. She's telling me, Michelle, to tell you that she has the baby. Do you understand?' Michelle burst into tears.

'She says to me that you have spent the last 12 years trying to get on with your life, but you have never had closure. Closure from the baby's crossing. Your daughter wasn't a miscarriage she was a termination but the decision you had to make was not straightforward. There was something wrong with her skull, it hadn't formed properly and her head had been misshapen.'

Michelle began to sob.

'Yes,' she replied, 'Yes that's all true.'

'Now your grandmother tells me the child had to be born into the world and she was premature. She tells me she was 13 weeks into the pregnancy and if you hadn't taken the advice of the doctors at the hospital in Manchester, to terminate the pregnancy, then your child would have died anyway at full term. This would have been far more risky to your life and far more painful, as you were already aware of the outcome. Is this correct?'

'Yes it is,' Michelle sobbed.

'And it was necessary for you to have a funeral for your little daughter?'

'Yes, yes.'

'Your grandmother tells me your child was conceived at a very difficult time in your life. The gentleman in my dining room was not her father.'

'Correct,' Michelle said. 'Correct.'

Through the sound of her voice, I could sense that the emotion was building in her.

'Now who is Grant? Oh, can I re-phrase that? Grant is your ex, or someone who wasn't very nice to you in your life. Do you understand?'

'Yes.'

'Someone treated you very badly and destroyed your trust. Your gran's telling me this.'

'Yes, it was Grant,' Michelle confirmed.

'Your gran tells me you've been with this other man for a short while and you've settled a bit better.' Michelle nodded assent.

'She says you never could come to terms with the loss of your daughter.'

'No I couldn't, I couldn't. I just couldn't.'

'Now I have a girl joining me from the Afterworld. She looks to be around 12 years old. She has long curly, bright red hair and is quite tall. She's coming forward with some friends she tells me.'

'This girl says she's your daughter and she gives me the name Susan. Do you understand, Michelle?' I asked.

At this the grief which had built up inside Michelle for 12 years poured out. It was as if I had pulled the plug on a great reservoir.

'That's her name David – Susan – that's her. Oh God!'

'Now she's making me draw something for some reason.'

Susan was asking me to pick up a pen and paper and draw, so I did just that. She made me draw an oblong box, then an oval inside it and the outline of her head and shoulders with a piece of cloth covering her forehead. I couldn't work out what she was trying to make me draw, so I asked Michelle.

'Can you understand why she wants me to draw this? What is it? What does it mean?'

I lifted the drawing up to her. Again there was an outpouring of grief. I could sense it drowning me. The sorrow was overpowering. Michelle pulled out an envelope and then a card – oblong in shape with an oval cut out. Inside the oval was a picture of her premature baby, Susan. She was dressed in her little baby clothes. She looked as if she were sleeping. Susan had made me draw the card her mum had with her.

Susan said, 'Oh mum, what have you brought that for?'

Even I was starting to become emotional.

Then I told Michelle there was a little boy with her grandad, a miscarriage. He had been called Tom by the Spirits and he was hers. She admitted that she'd had an earlier miscarriage but was surprised that he had come through because she didn't think that mis-carriages could.

'Love you mum,' Susan said. 'Like your trainers, mum. They're new aren't they?' she queried.

I repeated what Susan had said.

'Yes they are. Oh, I'm so shocked.'

Michelle began to tremble.

'I'll tell you what, Michelle, let's ask her to show us or tell us about you. See if she's been watching.'

'Please do,' Michelle replied.

'Well, she's telling me you have a daughter, Elizabeth, who is Susan's sister.'

'Yes David.'

'And she's a Goth. She's telling me that Elizabeth is a Goth. She dresses in dark clothes and dyes her hair black. She's really arty; she likes to choose her own clothes.'

'Correct.'

'She's telling me she wants a tattoo.'

'Yes.'

'She says Elizabeth is older – 14 or 15. Is that correct?'

'That's quite right, David.'

'Susan thinks Elizabeth is very different from her. She listens to strange music.'

'She does, indeed,' Michelle agreed.

'So tell me Michelle, what does this tell you?'

'She's watching me, David.'

'Yes, she's never left your side. She still doesn't leave you. She is in the non-physical side of life. That's all.'

I could sense that Susan was getting restless.

'Can I go now please?' she asked. 'I want to play with my friends.'

'Just one tick,' I replied to Susan.

'Susan wants to go now; I think she's bored.'

'Oh?' Michelle said.

'I need you to understand something Michelle; kids are the same both here and in the Afterworld but your child was premature so didn't develop any characteristics. They grow and develop as they would have in life.'

'Is she happy then? I need to know that David, I need to know that she's happy.'

'Are you happy Susan?' I asked.

'Yes, I'm fine. I like those trainers, tell her.'

'Susan has replied, "I'm fine and I like your trainers."'

'I'd buy her a pair if she were here,' Michelle said, bursting into tears again.

'No need, Susan is fine in the other world. She can imagine the trainers on herself anyway, don't worry about that.'

'Can I go now?' Susan asked me again.

'Susan needs to go now – her friends are waiting for her.'

'Tell her I love her, please.'

'You just did, Michelle. She loves you too.'

Michelle and I stepped back into the dining room.

'Did you get what you wanted then?' her boyfriend asked.

'It was amazing, absolutely amazing. I can't thank you enough, David.'

Brian rang me a while later to say he'd reached home safely. He said Michelle hadn't said too much but he could sense her ease.

I can truly say it is sittings like this that make my job as a Spirit Medium worthwhile. May God bless Michelle always.

MY THOUGHTS
by Michelle

I first saw David Traynor at the Broadoak Hotel, I was so impressed with the way he had given the messages to other people, they seemed really surprised that he knew so much. Unfortunately, I didn't get a message that night but there were a hundred people there. I was desperate to hear a message from my daughter who has passed over. At the end of the night I spoke to David Traynor's assistant and asked if David did private readings. There was a long waiting list, but I thought seeing David would be worth the wait. I put my name, number etc., and wrote next to it the word "desperate" as I was told it may be prioritised. After a couple of months, as far as I can remember, I had a phone call to say that Mr. Traynor had had a cancellation and could fit me in. I was to make my way to his home to have the reading and his assistant very kindly offered to take us. We arrived and, after a few minutes, I went into the conservatory to see David and have my reading. I had taken a photograph of my baby with me, me and her father named her Susan, after my mum. I didn't tell David about this, I just thought if she came through to me the photo might help. David made me feel comfortable and explained that he can only tell me of anyone that comes through to me and can't make someone come through that I want. I understood what he meant. He told me he had a tall man coming through to me like a grandfather figure but not a grandfather. Straight away I knew it was Bill. He was bringing through a girl of around ten to eleven years old. Immediately, I knew it was Susan and I felt so emotional – he described her to me as having long, red, curly hair. He told me she liked the Scissor Sisters. These are things I didn't know about her which, neverthe-less, made me feel comforted. He told me her name and said "Susan" straight out, he then tried to describe how she died and what was wrong with her. He said he felt that it wasn't a miscarriage and that it wasn't a straightforward termination. He told me that he felt something was wrong with her head – that it hadn't formed properly. He said that he can't draw very well but he would try to draw what he is being shown. He drew a girl's face with a cloth over her head. That was the same picture I had with me in my bag. I was totally gob-smacked! He then told me that she was saying, "Oh mum, why have you brought that photo of me?" How could he know all these things? They were all true. He was telling me that Susan said to stop feeling guilty about her death, because I have been very low about that. He said she couldn't have survived and I had made the right decision.

When I was pregnant with Susan and had my 12 week scan, they found an abnormality and transferred me to St. Mary's, Manchester for a more detailed scan. I was told Susan had a condition called an "encephally" which is where part of the skull doesn't form properly and was told her brain was just floating in the sack and that only I was keeping her alive. Also if I went full term she would be dead as soon as she was born. The only thing was to have a termination. I had to give birth to her at 13 weeks as I had gone past the abortion time. I can't describe how mortified I was and I felt like I'd just let her go and couldn't do anything about it. She had her picture taken with the top of her head covered up, to hide the open skull. She was blessed. I carried round this guilt for years, wondering if I could have done something else. I could not accept what had happened – I was constantly crying, wondering and wishing about Susan. She is a part of my life; and when David talked to me relaying what Susan was saying to him it made me feel a whole lot better. Some of the guilt was lifted and that really helped with things. He told me that she didn't like her Dad, because of the way he had treated me and had made me feel. I'm no longer with Susan's Dad – we did split up after 15 years because of the way he was treating me, so I can understand why David told me that. David also told me that Susan was really happy with the bloke who I am with now, she really likes *him and that she's told David that we will get married. When he told me this, I thought there is no way on Earth we will get married, because about this time, me and my partner, Steve, had just been talking about marriage in a big way. He had had a bad marriage in the past and swore he would never marry again. I had told him I was madly in love with him and was so happy that I've found my soul-mate and I want to marry him one day. However, he told me straight and up-front, that he feels the same way about me, but he is definite he will never marry again. This information is important because David was adamant that we would marry and I thought, "No way on Earth would that happen!" A few weeks after David's session, me and my partner, Steve, went through a terrible ordeal, which I cannot talk about. This ordeal was so horrific it actually brought me and Steve closer together and, because we had stood together as one, we talked and talked about everything. Steve said to me, that he completely loves me, is in love with me and feels that he has never had the closeness in his past relationship like we have and he told me he would marry me – wholeheartedly. I couldn't believe it and referred, in my head, back to what David had told me. It seems funny how things turn out! David told me I have a daughter who is fourteen, which was also correct. He said that Susan was telling him; "with a bit of an attitude", that, "My sister is a Goth." Then Susan was pulling her face because she's* not *a Goth, but she says it's O.K. for her sister to be one. She said that she's always joining in laughing with me and my daughter Lizzie, when we are together – laughing and that. Lizzie, my daughter, is really funny and we do have lots of laughs and fun together. David also told me that I have another child in Spirit and he is here. It's a boy with red hair and he is a year older. All this is correct. I'd had a miscarriage a year before Susan, at around eight weeks. In the Spirit World they had been growing up and these ages were correct – everything told to me was accurate. He said that she is a typical kid, feisty and with attitude and that. They both have two other friends who they play with and that she wanted to go now. The whole experience for me to have contact with Susan was happy. I felt relieved I'd heard from her and that she was O.K. Also, I didn't realise that "Tom", as the boy had been named in the Spirit World, would come through. As I'd had a miscarriage I didn't realise it worked that way – that he could come through too. It was a double surprise. I'd like to see David again and see how my children are going on and what they are doing. I have more peace of mind that they are O.K. David told me of other relatives, which he asked me to check with the family because I didn't know of them. When I asked family members, like my mum, she was able to shed light on certain people mentioned to me. I think David Traynor is very precise and feel that he also put the messages across with compassion but also didn't try to cover up anything. He told me the messages just how they came to him. I think David must be a great success and feel that he really helped me with things I had stored in my head for a long time. I hope he continues with his readings and think he could be much help to lots of people. I'd like to thank him sincerely.*

David told me that Susan was sitting next to me at one point and I could feel it very cold – it was an unbelievable experience. I could feel something and felt comfortable, happy and not scared because it was my little girl. It was amazing. I thank David for his help.

Miss Michelle Dawn Ashton.

Chapter 5

Dawn, Daryl and Rebecca

Life was getting hectic and I needed to bring together this book *A Bridge to Angels* and I began to realise what a time-consuming task it was, I can tell you.

One of the stories I wanted to include was that of Dawn and Rebecca, for a number of reasons. First, to give hope to those who have lost a disabled child, to let them know that when such children cross to the Spirit side of life and their physical body is left behind, so too are their ailments and disabling conditions. They become free of the body that once held them prisoner. Second, to let everyone with disabled children know that spiritual communication can open the door to enable them to move forward with their lives.

Sadly, because I had made an error when writing down the telephone number of Julie, Dawn's friend, I was unable to contact her. So I turned for help in another direction; I asked Rebecca in the Spirit World for help in finding her mother and Rebecca didn't disappoint me, enabling me to re-unite mother and daughter in more ways than one as you will find out later on.

It had been another successful night of clairvoyance at the Broadoak; one of the high points of the evening was when a Spirit gentleman came through and acknowledged each one of his family and friends in front of me. There were seven or eight of them and he gave each one an individual message which was detailed and accurate. Each of them, becoming emotional as I spoke, accepted their message as correct. It must have been very comforting for each of them to know that their loved one was fine on the other side. At the end of the evening I sat at the back of the room, meeting and greeting people. As I looked up, there stood Julie, Dawn's friend. I was overjoyed and very surprised at the same time. My heartfelt thanks go out to Rebecca and you will learn why.

It's all go in my house, there's never a dull moment – someone is always knocking at the door. I was running ten or fifteen minutes late when my next sitting, two ladies, arrived. I apologised to them as I showed them into the dining room. Because of its long table and low lighting, when I take people into the dining room, I am sure it might, sometimes, appear a little creepy. The lady whose sitting I was finishing had commented, on her entrance, that we could hold a séance around the table.

One of the ladies introduced herself as Julie; she was radiant with smiles. She introduced the other lady simply as "her friend". I don't know whether it was a conscious effort to conceal her name but she did only say "this is my friend". Her friend smiled and said, "Hi". She seemed the opposite of Julie, she appeared to lack confidence, was shy and quiet. Little did I know that this sitting would turn out to be one of the most moving sittings I've ever had the privilege to conduct.

I brought the previous sitting to an end, said my farewells to my visitor and moved back into the dining room to chat with Julie and her friend. Julie chatted freely but her friend just acknowledged what I was saying with an occasional nod or smile. At the time, I thought maybe she was nervous or frightened. It's amazing how differently people are affected by the expectation of their sitting. The pair wanted separate sittings, so I asked Julie into the conservatory first. She received great evidence; she had lots of fun moments and she gained comfort from her loved ones on the other side. What I did notice about Julie was she kept jovial and light all the way through her sitting. Now, in hindsight, I wonder if she was preparing me for the sitting to follow. I shall not dwell on the details of Julie's sitting, but please know it was positive and she was happy with the outcome. As she left the conservatory she thanked me, 'I really enjoyed that,' she commented. I smiled and asked Julie's friend to come in and take a seat. As she did so, I was overcome with the strongest feelings of sadness. This lady was one of the saddest people I've come into contact with. I could feel her heart was heavy; her sorrow was deep-rooted. Sadness comes on many different levels; I just knew she had felt like this for a very long time.

As I started to link with the lady, an older gentleman stepped forward. He looked to be in his early 70s, quite a stout man, his hair thin on top. He made me aware he had a bad lung condition; his chest and breathing had been bad for several years before he crossed over. He told me he was Dawn's grandad.

'Who is Dawn?' I asked him.

He confirmed it was the lady sitting before me. Now the mystery was solved. Both sittings had been booked in Julie's name only and this lady's identity, until now, was not known to me.

Speaking to Dawn, I explained I had her grandad with me and described his appearance. I then added, '… and he tells me your name is Dawn.'

A still-subdued Dawn simply acknowledged, 'Yes.'

Her grandad confirmed to me she had had a sad life which, at times, had just been little more than an existence and that she really did deserve a better time. I repeated this to Dawn; she agreed the sentiment. Then her grandad pointed out, of all the losses of her loved ones she had experienced, three were major. He indicated to me he would try to help bring these people through to her.

Sometimes, some of our relatives open the doors for our other loved ones to come forward. It's a very common occurrence in spiritual communication.

So it was evident to me her grandad had been concerned with the way her life had been since he'd crossed over.

'Next, I am joined by a younger man, do you understand?' I said.

'Yes,' she replied.

'He makes me feel there were some complications with his crossing. Do you understand?'

'Yes, David I do.'

'Now he is showing me the police, he tells me he had a bit of a run in with them. He has just laughed; he said he could be a bit of an unruly type in life. I think he is joking though,' I added.

'No it's true, but he was not a bad person, just an innocent really. And the situation with the police is true also,' she replied.

'He is making me feel he is on a roof or high up. Then he falls and crosses over.'

'Yes, a roof. Not high up though.'

'O.K.,' I replied. 'There's confusion with the police though over this matter, either he was accidentally pushed when he tried to jump off the roof, or they said he committed suicide. Does this make any sense at all, please? Only, it feels a little jumbled to me.'

'It all makes sense, David. It's all correct. I know why you are saying what you are saying to me.'

Although Dawn had said what she had, in my heart, I knew something I'd said was jumbled. I wasn't making sense of some of the details.

'Can I just go back and try to get that detail a little clearer?' I asked.

'Yes,' she replied.

'He makes me feel he shouldn't have been up on the roof, or what he was doing on the roof wasn't right. And what happened on that roof didn't come out correctly at the inquest. That is, it's to do with suicide. Is this any clearer?' I asked still baffled.

'No, it was clearer to me before. Would you like me to tell you?' she offered.

'No thanks, *I* must tell you,' I retorted.

'He makes me feel he is your husband, and now gives me the name Daryl.'

'Yes, he is my husband and that's his name. He crossed over when he was young as you have said.'

'Oh great, that's great,' I said happily getting carried away. Then I realised. 'Oh, I'm sorry! I don't imply it's great about his crossing. I mean, I'm glad for you that it's making sense.'

Dawn smiled. She acknowledged that she knew what I meant. We Mediums have to be absolutely clear about every single detail. It is so important and vital to this work.

'He is now making me feel sorry for what happened. He takes me to a little girl. So you must have a daughter to him?'

'Yes that's correct.'

'He now tells me you are his heroine and he couldn't have coped with his daughter without you. I feel she was disabled in some way, to her spine. Yes, something was wrong with her spine; it was severed or wrong in some way,' I added. 'This was from birth too. Do you understand please?'

'Yes I do. She was born with spina bifida,' she replied.

'Now who is Becca?' I asked.

'My daughter, Rebecca,' she confirmed.

At this point, Dawn became emotional and overwhelmed by what I had said.

'She is here in the Spirit isn't she?'

'Yes,' she replied through her tears.

'Your husband says to tell you your daughter Becca is with him there.'

'Good,' she replied again.

'He is looking after her for you.'

The emotion now flooded out freely, 'That's what I needed to know, David,' she said.

I couldn't actually see Rebecca at this point but Daryl was speaking to me openly. Then suddenly, there she was smiling brightly. A lovely young girl, not very tall, aged about 20. Then she just said to me, 'I'm Becca. Tell my mummy I love her and I'm cured. I am no longer disabled, I am fine. Mum looked after me all by herself. She never had a moment to call her own. She never stopped loving me.' As Rebecca spoke her words I repeated them to Dawn. It was a very emotional time and, as I'm sure you will agree, every word was of paramount importance to her mum.

'Becca says you've been depressed with her passing.'

'It's so hard,' Dawn exclaimed. 'She was my life.'

'She says her nan and grandad were fantastic, Dawn.'

'She loved them so much, David,' she replied.

'Maybe you could get a little job or take a college course, Dawn, and take your mind off it all. It would do you good,' I suggested. 'It would help you meet new friends, it could be a new beginning,' I continued. 'Becca tells me you're the best mum in the world. Her crossing came suddenly and was a shock to you.'

'Yes,' her mother replied.

'She is taking me to her kidneys and her other organs. She tells me she'd had to see specialists all through her life and she'd had many operations.'

'Yes, that's right,' Dawn said.

'She says one of the specialists was from Manchester Royal Infirmary, do you understand?'

'No, that's wrong,' Rebecca's mum replied.

'Are you sure? She says it's correct.'

'Yes, I'm sure that's wrong, David.'

'Look, check it out. Becca tells me it's correct. Please find out and let me know,' I said. 'You know, I may have picked it up wrongly too. Maybe I've misunderstood that piece of information,' I added.

'I will check,' she promised.

'Now Rebecca is taking me to Cheadle, Swinton and Eccles for links with you. Can you recognise these links?'

'Yes, they are all correct.'

'Becca makes me feel Julie has been a good friend. She lives close by but not next door.'

'That's right.'

'She is now showing me sign language, I think it's referred to as "deaf signing", do you understand?'

'Yes, completely.'

'She shows me Blackpool and a photo of her and her friend. She is showing me line dancing, but it's not line dancing. Do you understand?'

'Goodness, yes; she did wheelchair dancing all the time.'

[David had said, 'line dancing' and this was corrected by Dawn to 'wheel-chair dancing'. It was only

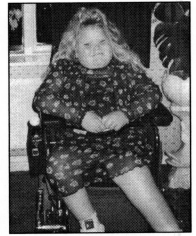

Rebecca who had love and tender care from her devoted family.

just before this book went to print that Kath, a friend of Dawn, noticed that Rebecca, on the photograph taken that day at Blackpool, was wearing a T-shirt bearing the legend, *Line Dancing*. The T-shirt was presented that day by the organisers and David must have picked up on that when he gave his reading.]

'She is becoming tired now. She wants you to know she loves you very much - she is shouting it. They must both step back now, love, but know your lovely child is safe with your husband.'

'Thanks for that David,' Dawn said quietly.

I turned around and made my way back into the dining room where Julie sat.

'Did Rebecca come through to you, love,' Julie asked.

'Yes,' Dawn replied.

'Good,' Julie exclaimed enthusiastically.

It was really funny, her confirmation sounded as though someone had baked a cake, she'd taken a slice out of it, tried it and liked it. It was a good and genuine reaction.

'Feel better, Dawn?' she asked.

'Yes, loads better,' she confirmed.

'Thanks, David,' they both said, on leaving the room and making their way to the front door.

'If we want to come again, may we?' Julie asked.

'Of course,' I replied and they left.

Here, I leave Dawn, Rebecca's mother, to tell her own story. It is a story of Dawn's strength and love for a daughter who was born disabled. I know that Dawn intended this account to be a tribute to Rebecca, but I believe it is also a deserved tribute to Dawn for being such an exceptional mother. These are Dawn's actual words.

I met Daryl when I was 22. Daryl was 17 at the time. We got along really well and it wasn't long before we started a relationship. Not long into the relationship I found out I was pregnant. We were both over the moon and decided to get married. We were going to be a family: Daryl, me and our much-wanted baby.

During the pregnancy I was very sick. People said it would stop after three months, but weeks passed and I found out I wasn't putting on any weight. My bump was growing, but I was actually losing weight. Additionally, I wasn't feeling much movement from the baby.

On my hospital visits the medical staff became quite concerned about my pregnancy and admitted me several times to monitor me and my baby. I only had two ultrasound scans – one at nine weeks and the other at 33½ weeks. One both occasions, the hospital staff said everything was normal, the baby was developing and growing normally as it should be. So any concerns that Daryl and I had were dispelled and we couldn't wait for our little bundle to arrive.

At 36 weeks my waters broke at home. After a long labour my baby was born via Caesarean section, after me being in distress. When I woke from the anaesthetic, a nurse was at my side telling me that I had a little girl but they thought there was something wrong with her. I asked what it was and she told me my baby had spina bifida and hydrocephalus. They had taken the baby to the special care baby unit for tests and I hadn't even seen her.

I was devastated. Daryl eventually came back to me. He had been with our little girl. He was over the moon with our daughter and told me how beautiful she was. I cried and said, 'What are we going to do? How will we cope?'

Panic was setting in. Daryl told me everything would be okay and together we could cope. He also told me that he had chosen a name for her whilst he had been watching over her – her name was Rebecca. The next three months went by in a blur. Our little Rebecca had 13 operations/procedures and we were constantly in and out of hospital. Daryl was a tower of strength and was true to his word when he said we would cope together – that's exactly what we did.

Two years and numerous hospital visits later, my world collapsed. The police contacted me and gave me the devastating news that Daryl had died. Apparently there had been an altercation between him and a police officer. A police investigation concluded that no blame could be attached to the officer. The inquest concluded that Daryl died of natural causes. I had to accept that my husband had died, aged 20, and now I had to get on with my life and bring up Rebecca alone.

My outlook was very bleak and I wondered how I was going to manage. It was extremely hard coping with Rebecca's needs. The care she needed was 24/7, but it was made easier because of Rebecca's character.

Despite her many disabilities she was a very happy, fun-loving and caring child. It was a pleasure to be in her company and the bleak moments when everything seemed too much were made bearable because of the way she was.

When Rebecca was 3½, I had a brief relationship with someone. This resulted in my becoming pregnant. Rebecca now had a beautiful sister, Rachael.

Rebecca had a full and varied life. She went to school and various clubs. One year she went to America with 'Destination Disney'. Another year she went to the Lake District with a youth club. One of her favourite trips was to Blackpool with the wheelchair dancers.

Two nights a week Rebecca went to the youth club. A taxi would pick her up and bring her home again. It was the same taxi driver every week. He was called David and Rebecca liked him a lot, as he would always have a laugh with her. Eventually David became one of my closest friends, my rock. It was through David that I met his sister, Julie. We got on from the first meeting. We were on the same wavelength and became good friends.

Rebecca's health started to deteriorate in October, 2004. She had fluid in her lungs and she developed a pressure sore which resulted in a long spell of bed rest and she became oxygen-dependent.

Her quality of life took a drastic turn for the worse in the summer of 2005. I was informed by her specialist that her heart was failing and at best she had two years left to live. In January, 2006, Rebecca developed pneumonia and the medical profession thought that I should tell her that she didn't have long to live. How does a mother go about telling her child she is going to die? There was no way I was going to do that!

Rebecca died on 23 February, 2006. She died peacefully in her sleep at home, aged 17. Her sister Rachael had gone into her room to see if she would like a pancake. Rachael came straight out of Rebecca's room and said she couldn't wake Rebecca. I knew immediately, that her time had come. I calmly went into her room. All I can remember was gazing down at my beautiful daughter and hearing Rachael screaming in the background. 'Wake her up Mum, wake her up.'

The weeks to follow were a blur and I just went through the motions of living. One day Julie arrived with a book written by David Traynor. She thought reading the book might give me comfort and, she was right, it did.

I asked Julie if she would like to go and see David for a private reading. She said 'Yes' and arranged a meeting for us both. When I had my reading with David, members of my family came through including Daryl, but not Rebecca. I was beginning to feel a little disappointed until David asked me who was 'Rebecca'.

'I've got Rebecca here and she's with her dad.'

At that moment relief washed over me because she was with her father. David went on to tell me that Rebecca liked Blackpool and that she was dancing – like line dancing, but it wasn't. Did I understand? I knew that this was the wheelchair dancing which Rebecca loved and this was a tournament she took part in, at Blackpool.

Rebecca told David to tell me that she liked the photo of herself and her best friend, Naomi, at Blackpool. She told him that I had put it up in the living room. I was stunned. Naomi's mother, Denise, had cut the girls from separate pictures and put them together to make one photo of them both wheelchair dancing. Denise had put it into a silver photo frame for Rebecca while she was still poorly. It now had pride of place in my living room.

David told me that Rebecca was doing sign language; did this make any sense? It made perfect sense because Rebecca had learnt it at school. One thing that puzzled me during my reading was David's reference to Manchester Royal Infirmary. This made me smile as it was as it was a hospital that we'd never been to. David was adamant that it was MRI as Rebecca had told him so. A few weeks later that I discovered that the particular doctor mentioned by David did indeed work at MRI.

My eyes filled with tears when David said Rebecca was singing
Simply the best *as it was her special song. She sang it with her*
nana (my mum).

I came away from seeing David much calmer than I had felt since
Rebecca's passing. My mind had been put at rest knowing that she
wasn't alone and was with her dad. David was touched by my
Rebecca's story and wanted my permission to use it in his new
book A Bridge to Angels. *I felt it was a privilege for my darling*
daughter's memory to be cherished forever in David's book.

I saw David again shortly after the meeting with Julie. During this
meeting something happened which blew me away. Julie and I
were sitting with David going through the details of the previous
reading, when Rebecca came through. She asked David if she
could give me a kiss. Julie and I just stared at each other in
disbelief, wondering how this could happen. David asked me if I
would be O.K. with this and, when I said I was, he explained what
it would feel like. He said that when Rebecca kissed me, it would
feel like someone blowing on my skin and it would feel cold.
Rebecca was getting impatient and just wanted to come over to me
as David kept telling her, 'O.K. sweetheart, just a minute. Just
wait a minute.' Eventually, David told Rebecca to go ahead. Tears
began to roll down my cheeks as David told me that Rebecca was
walking directly in front of me. David fell silent and I felt a very
cold sensation on my cheek and down one side of my body. It felt
as though someone had opened a 'fridge door and a blast of cold
air had touched my skin. I put my hands out to the side of me and
said, 'She's here at my side, I can feel it, I can feel her.' David
confirmed that Rebecca had moved to the side of the sofa, put her
hand on the arm of the sofa leaned over and had kissed my cheek.
This was the most amazing experience I have ever had and I am truly
grateful to David for helping Rebecca to come to me in this way.

Thank you, David, from the bottom of my heart. Thank you.

Dawn.

Chapter 6

Christopher

After Julie and Dawn had left, I sat in the lounge munching a caramel wafer and washing it down with a mug of hot coffee. Andrea had gone to bed, she wanted to read her book and relax. Barry had also retired to catch up on his sleep.

Time was ticking; I decided to watch a little TV before going to bed myself. My habit, no matter what time I finish my sittings, is to thank my Guides and the Spirit people who have joined and worked with me that evening. Afterwards, I'll eat a light snack and drink something, usually a glass of red wine. This physical action grounds me and helps me to stay closed down. Television can do that too. Sitting in my favourite chair near the window, I picked up the remote and pressed the "on" button. The picture displayed the famous face of Derek Acorah in the programme *Most Haunted*. Derek was in the middle of his exploration of an old pub. He was just in the throes of being "pushed" by a Spirit male who visited the building and had been sighted frequently. Derek's eyes were rolling and a very threatening voice was issuing from his mouth. The look on the face of the woman who co-presents the show was one of absolute horror. In a dishevelled state, Derek collapsed into the arms of some of the television crew members. They called out, 'Derek, come back. Derek, you O.K?' Eventually, he came round.

Someone always seems to be invading Derek's body. I'd be fed up with that. However, listening to Derek and watching his work unfold in front of me gave me no reason to disbelieve him or his particular gift of Mediumship. I believe there is so much to be discovered and understood about the Spirit World. If one man makes a statement of happening or fact in this particular subject, I believe it can only be taken as his point of view. So who am I to say what I am watching isn't truth, isn't real? I am no-one to pass judgement.

Well, little did I know that some time later I would get the chance to sample just how excellent the Spirit Medium Derek Acorah really is. I share that moment with you a little later on. But it was approaching midnight and time for bed.

Sometimes, communication yields only a small amount of evidence; at other times it can give you a great deal of detail, so that it seems as if one's loved ones are actually here in the flesh.

Do you remember Martin who featured in my first book? I can remember his mother Linda clearly and her saying at our first sitting, that his communication had been so clear and exact it had made her feel that he had been in the room at her side. By comparison, I've sat for a family four times now and some excellent information came through at first, then nothing. They still can't come to terms with the reality of communication; the whole situation is so difficult, it can be so frustrating at times.

I have reached the conclusion that some people find it harder to come to terms with the fact you can still communicate with their loved ones, after they leave the physical plane, than with their crossing – strange thought that. Nevertheless, a little knowledge and a lot of truth frees you and your mind.

It had been another successful evening at the Broadoak Hotel, Ashton-under-Lyne. Just as I was about to leave, a tall, attractive young woman with red, curly hair came up to me and suddenly broke down in floods of tears.

'I need help David,' she sobbed uncontrollably. 'I need help.' That's all she could say. A man stood behind her. He had a beard and moustache and seemed to be in his early 50s. He was calm and silent. They almost didn't seem to be together, but as she became more upset, he reached out his hand to comfort her. She was desperate. At one point she couldn't even speak.

'I wanted her so much. She never came. I go every day to her grave. Oh God, I can't go on.' I took hold of her hand.

'I wanted so much for her to come through,' she said, staring at me.

'I'm desperate to hear from my mother,' the girl exclaimed. At this point I tried to calm her down by asking her name.

'I'm Lisa,' she cried. 'This is for you,' and she placed a piece of amethyst into my hand. Again she became inconsolable and I knew how much she needed help. The crying went on for twenty minutes or more and I asked her to leave her telephone number and said I'd call her. She did this. I always know when there is a strong need for my services.

I arranged to see Lisa early the following week. Her sitting date and time arrived and so did she. I still had no clue as to who was the quiet gentleman who had escorted Lisa to my demonstration, but I was aware that he had driven her to my house. She was accompanied, this time, by a friend who she introduced as "Marjorie". It seemed to me that the two women were friends of long standing, or even relatives.

In actual fact, they had met each other just a few days before at the cemetery, but I only discovered this later. I asked Lisa to sit in my conservatory, but then a discussion started between Lisa, the gentleman and Marjorie about who was going to sit in on the reading. Time was ticking by and we were already ten minutes into the sitting time and had not even started yet. So I took over and suggested that they all sat in together. I normally allot an hour to each reading and I try not to run over, simply so I can have a little time for myself at the end of the evening. If it gets past ten o'clock, I have no time to talk to my wife, Andrea, and my friend, Barry, or to catch up with their news.

Marjorie seemed hesitant and a little nervous. She exclaimed, 'I only came to support you, Lisa'. But Lisa took up my suggestion and Marjorie was cajoled into going into my conservatory. Lisa sat at the back and the gentleman sat opposite Marjorie.

Lisa's mother came through, communicating strongly. Her mother said she was well and explained that Arthur, the quiet gentleman, had, in fact, been her partner. Her mother gave her name as "Barbara" and she sent her love to Lisa and Arthur. She spoke to Lisa and told her what she had been doing. She described the circumstances of her crossing into the World of Spirit and described events that had happened to her during the life she had shared with Arthur. Barbara was a first-class communicator.

She had not been long in the Spirit World and I could see clearly the relief on the faces of Lisa and Arthur. All through Lisa's part of the communication, as her emotions peaked, Marjorie became very attentive to her. It was lovely to watch. I've said this many times, but I will say it again and again – bereavement really can bring out the loving and caring side of human nature.

What happened next could not have been planned by anyone. But before I go on, I must explain something. During the month that preceded this sitting, I'd been made aware by my Guides that they would be asking me to sit for a special lady who was very much in need of my help. I was aware that what would unfold would be a tale of great sadness.

Marjorie sat quietly as I spoke to Arthur and Lisa. She was quiet, almost motionless, listening to what was being said. I couldn't see Marjorie's eyes which were obscured by a large pair of dark sunglasses. Afterwards, I felt sure they were placed there to block out the years of sadness she must have lived through, until the moment when, in my conservatory, all that sadness, turmoil and emotion would come to an end.

'Can I come to you now, Marjorie? I have a lady joining me. She tells me she is your mother – a very small, white-haired lady. She tells me that you took great care of her before she passed over to the other side of life. I'm joined also by William, Bill, your grandfather and by your father. He is smaller than Bill and bald. Do you understand?'

'Yes,' Marjorie answered looking shocked.

'I have a younger gentleman joining me, Marjorie. He crossed around the age of 20 years in a freak vehicle accident. He is tall and has dark hair. He is your son,' I exclaimed.

'Oh my God, I don't believe it,' Marjorie said out loud. 'I've waited all these years.'

Clearly, she was shocked by what I had said.

'Oh my Goodness, Marjorie! You are the next chapter in my book. My Guides are telling me this.' Jason, my main Spirit Guide, had pointed out that this situation had been planned by the Spirit World.

Lisa exclaimed, 'I can't believe this,' and just burst into tears. Marjorie looked totally stunned.

'I've only met Marjorie in the last few days,' Lisa explained. 'My friend and I had gone to put flowers on my mum's grave and Marjorie was putting a rose on her son's grave. The graves are close by.'

'Who is Chris?' I asked aloud.

As Lisa was saying 'That's his name,' Marjorie, at the same time, was exclaiming 'That's my son's name.'

Lisa continued through her tears. 'My friend and I knew Chris and we put some rose quartz crystals down on his grave for him. I saw Marjorie there and told her I knew her son. Then, I told her I'd been to see you at your Ashton-under-Lyne demonstration and I asked her to come along here tonight. I *knew* it was for a purpose.'

'It's been so long,' Marjorie kept repeating. 'I can't believe it, it's been years and years.'

'Your son, Chris, tells me that you have had an awful time in your life. He names a man who gave you a terrible time; and says you didn't deserve it. He says that your relationship is breaking down right now and he wants you to know he has been watching all that has gone on. He wants you to know he loves you so much.'

'Now he gives me the name of a Jane who is close to you, perhaps a sister, daughter, maybe a sister-in-law.'

'Yes, my daughter, his sister,' Marjorie confirmed.

'Well, Chris says Jane's problems are like history repeating itself. Her relationships haven't been too successful either and he says that Jane has never come to terms with his crossing over. He says they were very close when they were young. He wants her to know he is okay over in the Afterworld.'

'I still can't believe this. Is he telling you all this now, while I'm here, David?' Marjorie asked.

'Yes, that's why I can describe him, tell you about his crossing and tell you about your family and all that has gone on. He has never left you and has watched all this happening. Jane's happy now, he says. She's studying for a new career, or within a new career. Something she should have done years ago, he says.'

'Correct, it's all true,' Marjorie confirmed.

'Now he shows me throughout this trouble, this breakdown, there has been a move from a house to a flat.'

'That's me, I've moved out into a flat,' Marjorie said.

'He is saying that your life, Marjorie, was unhappy with this quiet man you lived with. Chris says he would love to see you enjoying yourself, having fun. But he says that wasn't happening.'

'That's right,' said Marjorie.

'He needs you to know he loves you Marjorie. He thanks you for what you have done and he is sorry his crossing was such a great shock to you. He is giving me a birthday around the first of September. Do you understand, my dear?' I asked.

'Yes, I do,' she replied.

'Now he has to step back. He has asked me to ask you to bring your daughter Jane. He would like to communicate with her.'

'Oh, I will phone her – it's just that she may find it hard to accept. She never speaks about it. She must bottle it up inside. I can only think that's what she does. She must feel it greatly, because they were so very close.'

'Tell her, Marjorie; let her know he wants to communicate and she will understand. Now both of you, Lisa and Arthur, I've got to stop. I hope that you can accept that your loved ones are well, on the other side of life.'

'I'm amazed,' Marjorie interrupted.

'I just knew when I met you that I needed to tell you about David,' Lisa repeated. 'Thanks, David,' Lisa offered.

The sitting came to an end. I could see a little queue forming outside the dining room. I'd gone over time by 40 minutes. Oh my, another late night – just what the doctor ordered!

I showed Lisa, Marjorie and Arthur to the door.

Christopher Tinning who died tragically on holiday in Majorca.

'Marjorie, I promise I'll phone you tomorrow,' I declared and, with that, they left.

The Spirit World moves in a most miraculous way. I had no clue that that sitting would turn out the way it did, but it was wonderful. I find it so exciting working for the Spirit World, not knowing what is going to be the outcome when I make communication with the other side. It's all part of my spiritual journey and I tread the path joyously.

As promised, the call was made to Marjorie. A date and time was set and – hey presto! – Marjorie and Jane duly arrived. I could see that Jane was nervous about the whole thing but I took to her straight away; she was very mild mannered and really "grounded". She had obviously braced herself for the sitting.

She did not, however, look as I had imagined her. She was quite small and thin with long, brown, wavy hair. I'd imagined her to be totally different.

'It's lovely to meet you Jane. Can I offer you some water or anything to drink as we are going along?'

Jane accepted and we began to settle in each other's company.

'Chris is here now, with me.'

'He is here now?' Jane echoed.

'Yes. He has just said "hello" to you both.'

'Now, I'm going to ask him for some evidence. He tells me there is a scooter and a car involved in this accident; that an old man is driving on the opposite side of the road.'

'Well it did involve a scooter, but we didn't know the other bit, about the man,' said Jane.

'Chris tells me he was riding a scooter. He'd been to see friends and an old, local man drove round the corner and his car veered off, over to the wrong side of the road, but my head hurts on this side and I feel as if I've just vomited.'

Jane was astounded. So was Christopher's mother. Both sat in front of me open-mouthed. 'Christopher is taking me to Palma, Cala d'Or, around that area.'

I have only been to Majorca once and, strangely enough, it was to Cala d'Or. It was a lovely place although it did rain a fair bit while we were there. When we came back, both Andrea and I looked like sheets of paper; pure white. We got out of the taxi, put our suitcases in the hall and took ourselves straight to the sun-beds in the local suntan centre. It had rained on and off for the whole seven days we were there, so that's how I remember Majorca – wet. Fortunately, it had great karaoke bars!

Neither of these ladies said a word. Both seemed too stunned.

'Now Christopher is making me aware that there is a birthday imminent, in the next few days. Do you understand?'

Marjorie seemed not to hear me but Jane just looked at me and said 'Yes', then burst into tears – the repair had finally begun for her. I was so glad. She deserved some peace in her heart.

'There was a reason for him mentioning Palma. This freak accident happened in Spain.'

'Yes,' Jane replied, again shocked.

'Christopher keeps talking about a party. I just can't get that detail from him, but he says he was offered a party or didn't want to have a party. Do you understand this?' I asked.

'Yes,' Marjorie replied. 'Chris didn't want a party for his birthday. He decided to go on holiday with his friends instead. He went on holiday to celebrate his birthday and never came back.'

Each word she uttered caused her pain. Why should lovely people go through all this heartbreak? It's so unfair, but I suppose it's life isn't it?

'He tells me he was going out with his mates and he'd only had a little bit to drink.'

'We didn't know that,' Jane said.

'He says he was on the way back when it happened.'

'Yes, that's correct,' Jane replied.

'Now Jane, he tells me that he sees you have been let down quite a bit and it's been hard for you and he has watched. He says you now have four children.'

'That's true,' Jane said.

'Did you call one after him? He is saying one has his name. Do you understand?' I asked.

'Yes, correct.'

'He is very flattered, he says. It's a great name, but he tells me someone wasn't happy with your choice. They said it was very morbid of you to call your child after your brother who had died so tragically. He says it was cruel and insensitive of them and they had no right to say this to you. He thinks it was a lovely thought and he thanks you.'

Jane wept again.

'Chris says you are nursing now, you have just started and he is glad to see this. He says you should have done it years ago, but you put it off and now, as you are really happy and settled, you have decided it's for you.'

At this point Jane let out a gasp. I believe the reality of my communication was beginning to register with her.

'I can't believe this,' she stammered.

'What can't you believe?' Marjorie said.

'That David is telling me things he couldn't know.'

'Well, Chris is telling him, that's why.'

I just laughed. 'Jane, trust me, it is Christopher. I wouldn't know these details about you and your life, would I?'

Jane just looked astounded.

'I feel Christopher was a clever lad. I want to say university standard.'

'Yes,' Marjorie replied. 'That's right.'

'This lad was quiet and academic. He says, Joan's not well; she couldn't bring you here tonight. Do you understand?'

'Yes, we do,' Jane replied.

'Oh, you have links here, with this area. Chris is making me look out of the window – you have links with this neck of the woods.'

'Yes, my friend lives just around the corner,' Jane replied.

'Oh, you have a pendant too, with "Chris" inscribed on it, he says.'

'Yes, I have.'

'He says your mother – you Marjorie – were there at his side, you went to him when this all happened.'

'I did,' she said sniffling.

'He says he is not too keen on Gary, but he loves Peter. He calls Peter, "Peter the Great", and says that Peter *is* great and that he really likes him because he makes you happy. So whoever Peter is, I know he makes you happy. Chris says there is someone around you who also calls Peter (whoever Peter is), "Peter the Great".'

'Well, David, Peter is my partner. Yes, I'm happy with him, I am more settled than I've ever been and yes, we do call him "Peter the Great".'

'He goes on to say there have been problems with your digestion, Jane. You have had a camera down your throat but now you're getting better. He says he has sent you healing and been at your side throughout. He says you were very, very concerned at one time that the problems with your digestion were much worse than they turned out to be. He wants you to know he has been there with you, at the doctor's surgery, the specialists. He says you have had bouts of depression too. He believes these problems with your health, together with his loss, will help to make you a truly great nurse because of all your experiences in the past.'

Jane said nothing. She merely looked flabbergasted as Christopher gave me all this information.

'There are also connections with Andrew, Jean and Mike. It was Jean who wasn't happy about the namesake business. True?' I asked.

'Correct,' Jane replied.

'He says you have taken some exams, Jane. He has printed "CONGRATULATIONS" over your head. That's lovely of him, isn't it?'

'Yes,' replied Jane.

'He is going to make his way over to you and your mum. You will feel his presence strongly and in addition it will go very cold around you – it's like someone blowing on you. Please don't be afraid,' I said calmly.

'Oh, my goodness,' Jane exclaimed, 'he has just touched my face ... now my leg.' She began to cry.

'Chris has just printed "TINY" over your head. Can you understand why he has done this?'

'That's what they called him, David,' Marjorie replied.

'I'm absolutely amazed,' Jane said. 'I never thought this would happen. I've heard about people like you, David – but you could never know all that information – the names, everything, were spot on.'

Marjorie and Jane had received strong communication. We talked more openly about Chris after the sitting. They also asked Chris some questions which were very personal and cannot be divulged. It was a lovely evening we had spent together and one I'll never forget. Chris stepped back, leaving his love with his mother and sister. As it happened, his mother had brought some poetry that Chris had written. I loved this particular poem and I'll cherish it and, with their kind permission, I've inserted it in this book for you all to enjoy.

After the poem, Christopher's mother will take up the story and fill in the gaps. Stories like this make me feel so humble that I have been chosen to communicate and be a Bridge to your Angels.

POEM

Why does the world go round?
Why are the trees green?
Who or what are we?
Why did we come about?
Is there life after death?
If God created us all equal
Why do people starve?

Is the disease Aids God's, or the Creator's
Way of saying it's wrong?
Why is there famine?
Why is there war?
Are nuclear missiles necessary?
Are we on a path of self-destruction?
What came first, the chicken or the egg?
The Bermuda Triangle?
Is there a hell?
Is there an end to a rainbow?
Does the Loch Ness monster exist?
Do plants have feelings?
Is the sky blue?
These questions and more
To be answered soon
Or will they be answered?
Who will answer them,
Me – You – someone afar?
Or will it be too late?

*The conclusion drawn to this sheer nonsense written by this
mentally-deranged teenage idiot is – nobody knows and, seriously,
who wants to know? YOU.*

*Winning a nuclear war means never having to say sorry – would
there be a winner?*

Christopher Tinning
August 1986

*On Sunday 3 August, 1986 Chris went to Spain on holiday to meet
up with his friends, who had already been there for a week.
Then on Wednesday 6 August, I decided to spruce his bedroom up
and freshen up the paintwork. The previous day I had sorted his
room and tidied things away. I wish I hadn't.*

Just after lunch, Arthur came home after finishing a job earlier than usual. Soon afterwards a young policeman rang the door bell. I came downstairs to answer the door and the policeman asked if he could come in. He looked uncomfortable and paused before saying, 'Your son, Christopher, has been killed in an accident in Spain.' The full details were still quite unclear and we were given the Foreign Office number and also those of the British Consulate in Palma and the travel company in Manchester, which had arranged my son's holiday.

In a daze, I walked the policeman to the door and thanked him for coming to let us know. Arthur and I just clung to each other in total disbelief. It couldn't be possible, not my Chris, not my level-headed, responsible son. He was *going to return to me and Jane his sister and we loved and needed him here with us, it had to be a mistake, it just must be.*

All of a sudden, I decided to defrost the fridge-freezer. Why?

I had to keep busy and Arthur started helping me because when that task was finished everything would be okay.

Minutes later, Chris's girlfriend and her mother came to the door very upset and shocked. Apparently one of the boys from Spain had phoned England and told them. They stayed until late afternoon. Jane still did not know what had happened. Arthur telephoned her boyfriend whom we knew would be going to meet her from the nursery where she was doing her work experience. When she got home, it was heartbreaking and she was inconsolable. 'Let's go and bring him home,' she kept saying over and over.

A short while later, a neighbour and friend came round and by this time, after Arthur had made umpteen phone calls to relatives, I started to go very cold, despite the warm weather. I couldn't stop shaking and my friend called the doctor.

A lady doctor arrived and sat down with Jane and myself and tried to calm us down. After a while she went, leaving a prescription for me for Ativan. *I never saw the doctor again. I had no back-up whatsoever. The phone never stopped ringing, everyone in disbelief. We eventually went to bed, the pain and grief overwhelming.*

The next day my youngest brother, Jim, and his family came over. They were very surprised to see I had made them all a meal, as if everything were normal, but I seemed to be in a bubble to keep away the grief. As long as it didn't burst, I wouldn't have to face the truth. Jim took the responsibility of phoning the various telephone numbers we had been given. All I wanted to do was to get to Majorca, but it was not so easy. Because it was the time of the summer holidays in August, flights were not easy to arrange.

When we phoned the police in Palma we were told that families did not often come over when accidents had happened and often the police said they sorted out the funeral (as such), there. We were frantic. My brother rang the Foreign Office for help and they said it was especially difficult to get to Majorca at that time as Prince Charles and Diana and their children were on holiday with the Spanish Royal Family. This meant nothing to us whatsoever. We rang the British Consulate again – they weren't of much help. Eventually, after numerous calls in an attempt to acquire tickets, my brother managed to get two tickets through the travel agents that Chris had travelled with. They did more than the British Consulate and the Foreign Office put together. Sadly, we couldn't get another ticket for Jane, who was distraught and said she was frightened we wouldn't come back either. It was one nightmare after another. Also, at this point, we still were not sure exactly where Chris was.

It was decided that Jane should go and stay with her nana. Arthur and I were driven to Birmingham Airport by two very good friends during the night – this was the last resort. I don't remember boarding the plane and I don't remember arriving at Palma. A kind young lady courier who worked for the travel agent met us at Palma and drove us to a hotel up in the hills.

We were told to stay near the room's telephone and when there was more information we would be informed. The next day, the travel rep phoned us, but we still didn't know where Chris had been taken to. I was taking the Ativan *as if they were* Smarties *and pacing the room like a headless chicken – the waiting and the not knowing were unbearable.*

On the second day, the rep rang us again and said Chris was in a mortuary quite a few miles away and a taxi was being sent to take us there. The mortuary was on the top of a hill, in a beautiful setting, and as I got out of the taxi, I started to shake with dread and fear. The rep waited outside.

Strange as it seems, I thought that now we had found him, we would be taking Chris back home with us. But this was not allowed. I was distraught because I thought everything was cut and dried. We returned to the hotel and again were told to stay near the telephone. The following day, there came another phone call telling us a taxi would be sent to take us to the police station in Palma and we could collect Chris's belongings.

We sat in the corridor there, and waited and waited. Eventually we were called into an office and given forms to fill in confirming who we were. An officer brought in Chris's suitcase. My heart seemed to be ripping apart.

Our experience at the police station was awful. We were treated in an impersonal and callous manner. It was as if we had gone to collect a trivial piece of lost property.

We returned to the hotel with the suitcase; I couldn't stop thinking that this was all I had left of my precious son.

On Thursday 14 August, 1986 the emotion I felt when we got home was indescribable. We brought Jane home from my mother's.

When Chris's friends eventually came home, they told me that as soon as they were told what had happened it was their intention to return home immediately, but they couldn't get an earlier, re-arranged flight. They came to see us, shocked and upset. No-one spoke much at all.

After a couple of weeks, during which numerous phone calls were made we were told Chris would be brought home by air freight. We had not been allowed to bring him home with us, which we presumed would happen.

The next nightmare we had to face was that when Chris was taken to the local undertaker's, it wasn't possible for him to be kept there, because the conditions were not adequate, so he was transferred to

Tameside Hospital Mortuary. I was inconsolable because I was not allowed to see him. A couple of days later, the Coroner from Stockport came to visit us and tried to explain the situation to us as gently as possible, leaving out the obvious reasons, which meant nothing to me – I wanted to take Chris home and sit with him, something I could not do in Spain.

After much soul searching, I decided that Chris should be cremated. My father had died the previous February, five months before Chris. Chris had remarked to me at Dad's funeral that he thought cremation was better than burial and that he would prefer it for members of his family.

Tuesday 26 August. It was three weeks after Chris's death that his funeral finally took place. Because we were not allowed to see him, the undertaker arranged for the coffin to be brought to our house so that we could sit by Chris's side until it was time for the funeral. Hundreds of people were there. We didn't realise he had so many friends and lots of them we didn't even know. We decided that we wanted to come straight back home after the funeral and we invited everyone who wanted to, to come back to the house.

How could I hire a room and celebrate his life, his life was cut short and taken so suddenly and tragically when he was at the start of a happy and fulfilling time?

Unbeknown to us, Chris's friends had had a collection in the pub where Chris used to drink. They had all put in their week's wages. They came to see me and handed me an envelope. We were overwhelmed by this gesture and told the lads that the money would be used to buy Chris's headstone.

It was my brother who suggested that we have a gravestone and bury Chris's ashes in the cemetery, then there would be a definite place where I could go and talk to him. I am so glad that I did this, because there I can let all my emotions flow without Jane seeing how upset I am all the time. Jane has had lots of problems and much heartache herself and sadly – thanks to Ativan and the doctor – I was in another world myself and not of much use to anyone.

We had to have a second small funeral on 28 August, 1986 for the burial of Chris's ashes – a funeral car for the ashes, a grave digger, the minister, myself, Jane, my mother, Arthur, Jim and his wife Marie and Chris's girlfriend, Jackie. It was all a haze. 'Please let this be over,' I kept thinking, 'then we will be back as we were before all this happened.' The whole situation was so unreal and painful to me.

Finally, there came the realisation that nothing was and never will be the same again without our Chris.

Marjorie Tinning

Since seeing David I feel so relieved because I had so many pent up feelings of sadness and devastation that I knew no-one would ever understand the depth of my sorrow. After speaking to David I feel like a huge weight has been lifted, even though the heartache goes on. David has brought me so much nearer to my wonderful son, Chris.

Marjorie Tinning.

When my mum told me she had been to see David Traynor and that my brother had come through, I was a bit sceptical. My brother died in August, 1986 due to a motor bike accident whilst on holiday.

Since my brother had died I had been to see a few mediums hoping that one of them would be able to give me some answers. My mum and I went to see David and he explained that Chris may come through but, Chris was always a bit shy, so I just sat waiting. David then told us that a young man has joined us and he described Chris so accurately that it couldn't have been anyone else.

He told me that Chris said he was glad I was finally doing my nurse training, which was something that I had wanted to do for ages. There was no way that David could have known this as this was the first time I had ever met him. He told me about my four children and about my partner, which was astounding. There were so many things that I wanted to ask Chris, that I hadn't had the chance to ask before he died. David told me that it was definitely my brother who I was talking to. I cannot thank David enough for what he has done for me after 21 years of not really knowing what happened to my brother. I now feel at peace and knowing that Chris is always around me and my children is a great comfort.

Thank you, David, for showing me that your loved ones are never far away.

Jane Tinning

Chapter 7

Talking to old friends

Children play a very special part in our lives, as I am sure you will agree and whether they are here in the physical life or on the other side, in the Spiritual World, their love for us and ours for them has no boundaries.

It was rapidly approaching a special time for me, my 40th birthday. Strangely, I still feel like a teenager, but when I look back at photos of myself I can see that I've expanded a little. It really is a true saying, age does creep up on you!

I'd decided to hold a party for my family and friends. The arrangements were in place and going ahead as planned. I'd been a little pre-occupied during the week leading up to the party with several different scenarios. I'd promised my good friend, Elaine, that I would arrange a fund-raising demonstration for a children's orphanage in Africa. Most of the children there are under five years of age and dying of AIDS. Elaine raises money for the orphanage; I admire her greatly for what she does. The demonstration was on the Monday before my party and it had been a sell out, which meant that Elaine could pay for more repairs to the orphanage, or give the children meat in their diet for a month, or the money could go towards air fares – remember that Africa is a long way away.

The demonstration had gone well; people were astounded by the level of communication and the amount of information that came through for them. A young man called Paul had linked in with me. He told me he had gone over to the Spirit World in a motorbike accident. He had been married only a few months previously. He was a chatty young man. The fact that he was audient to me, so I could hear clearly what he was saying, was especially helpful.

He directed me to a lady sitting at the back of the room with her friend. The young lady immediately acknowledged him, replying

'Yes, I know him. Yes, I know Paul and his family,' when I approached her.

I described him in detail and she acknowledged everything to be correct. All the time I was communicating with Paul I knew I had met him previously – on this side of life. When I had passed on his messages to the young lady, I returned to him in the Spirit, asking what was our previous connection. He revealed that he had worked at my hairdressing salon for six months, when he was 16 years old. I was then 19. He had been my apprentice. I was thunderstruck. 'Paul, I am so sorry. I didn't recognise you, my humble apologies,' I said sincerely.

He laughed and started to place in my mind memories of a rather rude situation that had happened in the salon when he had been there ... but I can't elaborate here. Paul said his good-byes and left. It was nice to see him again. We'd not got on well as young men; maybe it was that I had been very fussy about everything. It was my first salon and I aspired to be as successful as Vidal Sassoon.

A few days later, Paul approached me again as I was sleeping and informed me he would be joining the team which works with me in the Afterworld. I was overjoyed; I would have another chance to work with Paul. This time, I'd have some respect for him and treat him as a colleague, not as someone inferior. I believe it was my own immaturity which had been responsible for the failure of our relationship in the physical world. I was determined that things would be different this time.

Apologies from me were accepted by Paul and he has worked with me and my team in the Afterworld ever since; we get on well. However, back to my week. I have two lovely nieces and two nephews who had clubbed together to buy tickets for Andrea, Barry and me to see Derek Acorah at the Floral Hall, Southport. Kate, my eldest niece and David, her fiancé, agreed to come along too. I was so excited. I am always interested in watching other Mediums' work and am pleased when they are successful. I never feel envious and I'm grateful for that attribute. The Floral Hall was full to bursting. There must have been more than 1,000 people present. Our seats were right at the back but we had a good view.

Derek was lively and energetic. His messages were strong. It was clear to me that he was a very experienced Medium and I enjoyed the whole experience. Then came the best part of the demonstration for me. Derek stood in the centre of the aisle gesturing up to the area where we were seated.

'I have a lady here with me. She's a small lady with lovely white hair. She's called May Brennan. Who knows May, in the Spirit World, please?'

I knew immediately who she was. I'd been her hairdresser since I came out of college. She was one of the nicest people I ever met. In her later years, my mother had been accustomed to collecting and bringing her to my shop for her hairdressing appointments. Confidently I replied, 'That's me. I know May Brennan.'

I was handed a microphone. Derek stood at my side in the aisle. 'There's been a change in your premises recently – your premises, where you work,' Derek announced.

'Yes, that's correct.'

'It's been hard, very hard and very stressful I'm told.'

'Correct, Derek.'

'May says your new shop is lovely and she's watching and visiting it all the time.'

A little tear formed in my eye. That was such a lovely thought. I did like May; she was so patient and kind.

'Now, May tells me there was a little accident in the salon just recently, involving water. Do you understand?'

'Yes, it's true,' I replied smiling. I didn't tell Derek what the accident was or give any details, I wanted him to tell me, but I'll tell you all. Barry had turned a shower on in the back wash area in the small salon. The room was full of customers and staff at the time and the shower head had turned over, spraying water over everyone – and I mean everyone. I was soaking wet. Fortunately, everyone found it funny and laughed – it was a good job really. I had just stood in the centre of the salon, waving my arms about crying, 'No, no this can't be happening. No, no turn it off.' What a total fool I must have looked.

Derek said openly, 'The water soaked everyone, May says, she was laughing at the situation. She thought it was so funny.'

'Thanks, Derek,' I replied.

The next part of Derek's message was very poignant and significant to me and it's one of the reasons why I have included the story in my book.

'The Spirit World wish me to say to you sir, that you are an ambassador for them here to our Earth. You sir, are a Bridge for them, please know you have been chosen.'

I could do nothing more than stammer my thanks.

Wow, what a spiritual birthday present! This was the second time it had been acknowledged by another Medium that I would be a bridge from this life to the Afterlife and vice versa.

I was elated by my message. It may be that you wonder why I was so elated, since I am a Medium myself. Well, I'm only human. Wow, out of over a thousand people, I got a message!

When we arrived home it was late. Andrea and Barry sat chatting in the living room so I decided to go into the conservatory to meditate. They had decided to watch a science fiction programme on television – I think this might have had something to do with my decision. I can't stand subjects like that, I'd rather chew nails.

As I went deeper into my meditation I was joined by a boy, around the age of ten or eleven. He had a shiny bald head, quite round features and spoke with an Oldham or Bolton accent. He gave me two names, "Mark" and "Andrew". Strangely, his voice was very weak. It kept fading although I could see him clearly. The situation was a bit like tuning into Radio Luxembourg – I'd get some of his information, then other statements were missed.

I called my Guides for help. Jason tried but I felt the fault could have been mine, my mind was still with the Derek Acorah message. I don't think I was properly focused, fully aware. The boy kept giving me the two names, Mark and Andrew. Then he told me he had had leukaemia, which was incurable. Next he wished me a happy birthday. How strange, I thought, a stranger, a complete stranger wishing me happy birthday.

Then he started to image a caravan site to me. I recognised it from my younger days. It was Shaw Hall, just outside Southport, not far from where I live now. My mum still has a static home there. We have always had connections with that site, except for a short period when I was about 14 years old and was reaching the point where I didn't want to visit it any more. So mum and dad sold up for a while, but they always kept in contact with their friends there. When dad crossed over 16 years ago, I talked my mother into buying another caravan at Shaw Hall. She has good friends there and it would mean she could get away at the weekends. This she did and has never regretted it.

But the young man was showing me the caravan park as it was when I was young – the stream running through it, the bridge where all the youngsters congregated, the willow tree, the sand pit and the swings. It was truly amazing. Then he uttered the words, 'Remember me?'

You know, no-one would believe it, but it's a fact that I have the most awful memory – don't know what day it is sometimes; getting old you see.

He made me aware that he had a brother to the Earth plane. It was terrible of me, but I just couldn't remember him.

Then gradually, a distant memory rose up of a young boy and his brother who used to visit their grandparents' caravan during school holidays. I didn't have many friends at the time and I struck up a friendship with him and his brother. I must have been seven or eight years old. Vaguely, I remember asking the lad what had happened to his hair and in a matter-of-fact voice he had replied, 'I have an illness, I'm going to die soon.' But being a child myself and a very immature, naive child, I might add, I just said, 'Oh, O.K. then. Coming to play in the sand pit?' and that was that.

Then he showed me the caravan he used to visit. Standing behind him were two familiar figures – those of his nan and grandad. It was the same boy and the same adults; I could remember them but, sadly, not their names.

In this sort of situation, if I start to rack my brain too much I begin to weaken my link, it becomes polluted by my own thoughts and I can lose contact. I wanted to carry on communicating with him. Then – which I found so helpful and at the same time very moving – he started to show to me different events which had happened to me during my life, poignant situations, from being young and meeting him, almost to date. After each one he said the word, "Remember".

I was taken back to happenings like leaving school, getting my first shop, my wedding day – it was absolutely awesome. He must have watched me grow up and stayed with me for some reason. Maybe one day his family will approach me and want to speak to him. I don't know, I just suppose that's the reason.

His conversation seemed to last for minutes, in fact, it had lasted over an hour. Checking the time, as I finished my meditation, I found it was just gone midnight. The house was silent, except for the faint sound of Barry snoring as I walked along the landing.

I see that lad often now when I open to the Spirit, although not so much to talk to these days; as I'm usually communicating for others. Some Mediums believe you shouldn't communicate with Spirit people during meditation, their argument being that meditation is for personal benefit and communication is for the benefit of others. I can accept this, but I say it's my choice whether I communicate with someone during my meditation and my choice if I don't. If I don't like the look or sound of them, believe me, I cut the link immediately.

Shattered, but excited after the best birthday evening I'd ever had, I slipped into bed. It's a pity I couldn't have slipped into sleep soon after. The atmosphere in the bedroom was electric; it danced around and little lights, like small balls of energy (we call them orbs), came and went – it was my own spiritual fireworks display. Although just a little late in the day for me, especially when I had to be up the next day for work.

My birthday treat was over. I must have slept at some point. The next thing I remember was Andrea's mobile phone alarm going off. It was 7-45, nearly time to get up.

Chapter 8

Matthew

Barry suggested that we make a weekend visit to his parents in Essex. Secretly, I think he had been missing them. In the past, he had seen them much more regularly but, at this time, he was so busy it had been impossible for him to arrange a visit. It's a little different for Andrea and me; our parents live close by, we can see them every day if we choose.

Barry telephoned his folks, knowing that they would be overjoyed to see us all and his mum and dad, Pam and Alf, love having us there. In addition, they are very interested in the spiritual side of life and are always keen to know every detail of what has gone on since we last visited.

More often than not, whilst I am down in Essex, I combine the visit with a fund-raising event for Lions Clubs International charities, specifically Pam and Alf's local club to which they belong. This time, sadly, the notice was too short to put on such an evening, but it was still worth the trip to catch up with Barry's family.

Essex is about a 4½-hour journey from us. I usually drive, guided by my sat. nav., while Barry sleeps and Andrea drifts in and out of sleep. I drive because I'm a terrible passenger. However, we do stop *en route* for a meal to break up the journey.

It was 10-30 in the evening when we hit the lovely Essex countryside (although we couldn't see it at that time of night) and the village of Kelvedon, just outside Tiptree – jam country. We'd come through rain, heavy hailstones, mist, then more rain. Finally we arrived at Pam and Alf's and the sky was dark but very clear with lovely, twinkling stars overhead. As we pulled up on their driveway, the front door opened and Alf stood there to greet us. Then Pam appeared. The sky was so starry it prompted me to joke, 'Any room at the inn, please?'

Pam replied, 'Only the stable. Will that do?' We burst out laughing.

We were made welcome with the usual hugs and a bottle of red wine. Just what the doctor ordered after that long and boring journey.

Sitting down, we began to chat, catching up on all that had happened since our last visit. We booked a table for seven on the Sunday evening, at a local restaurant – for Barry and his parents, his sister, Belinda, brother-in-law, Simon, Andrea and me.

Sunday night went well. We had an excellent meal and a good chat. Simon and Belinda were relaxed and we joked and laughed. I had begun to feel a little strange, almost dizzy, throughout the meal. As this feeling began to come over me, Simon, without knowing I was feeling like this, said, 'Do you know, I'm buzzing and hot when I come near you, David. Look at my hands.' His palms were bright red and heat just flowed from them.

He must have repeated this comment four or five times. We just all laughed, but I truly believe it was making Simon feel a little "freaked out". After the worst bit of the evening was over – I mean paying for the meal – we all left for the car park. Just before reaching my car I felt light-headed, as if I were there physically, yet detached mentally. I recognised that I had been joined by one of my Spirit guides. His name is Pierre Rachén – he had been a Parisian artist when he walked the earth plane. He is a wonderful guide, giving timely advice and being full of fun. Pierre's messages were mostly for Barry by using his own knowledge of art to give guidance to Barry, who is a Spirit Artist. Barry must have realised that I was having a "funny turn" and he rushed over to support me in case I should fall forward, but I was in control. Through me, Pierre spoke and told us there was a need for the Spirit Guides to speak to us all. He wanted us to go home and relax and the Spirit would come through and all would be explained to us.

Pierre stepped back and I came back to myself. It always amazes me what goes on. Often, "spiritual" people say, 'No this can't happen. That can't happen.' I don't believe anyone really knows what can and cannot happen. The Spirit World's parameters are probably boundless. I believe that the reason why some of the established churches shun communication with the Spirit World is because they don't know enough about it.

Two minutes later and I was back to normal and we were making our way to Pam and Alf's, all wondering what was going to happen and what we were going to discover.

Having her priorities right, Pam put the kettle on while I threw myself down into a comfy armchair. I think they, like me, were wondering exactly what was going to happen. The atmosphere was a little tense. I must have nodded off, which is not unusual for me; I can sleep on a wire these days.

As I nodded off, my mind, I believe, was still very active. Although I was still half-conscious of my surroundings, I was transported to another plane, finding myself sitting by a blazing fire surrounded by Indians, North American Indians. I have to admit that, at one time, when I heard talk of Indian Guides called "Red Cloud" or listened to statements such as "there's a grizzly bear watching over you," I thought it was all rubbish. How wrong I was! I believe every word of it now. I was really there, at that moment, with the Indians.

Whilst I was having this great dream (as I thought at the time), Andrea, Barry and his family were witnessing a much different aspect of my experience. I had, apparently, begun to chant loudly, like a Red Indian. This chanting came to an abrupt end after two or three minutes, then my Guide, Jason, came through to the family and asked Belinda and Alf to sit next to each other. Addressing Barry as "doorkeeper", Jason requested him to sit at my side. Then Pierre stepped forward. He described a whole list of problems that Alf and Pam had been experiencing both in their personal life and also in health matters. They obviously knew about these problems; I did not.

One problem was Alf's breathlessness due to his body's reactions as he had recently stopped smoking – obviously a shock to his system.

Next, the Guide turned to Belinda. He told her she was desperate to have a child and had been for a long time. Pierre explained that the Indian medicine man would come through and very intense healing would be given to Pam, Alf and Belinda. At that point Belinda became very emotional – as if her feeling of desperation, which had been bottled up for years, had suddenly been released. The Guide added that she would soon conceive a boy, one has been here on Earth many times before in many different incarnations.

Belinda, being Belinda, asked Pierre if she would be a good mother. He replied, 'Yes, a very good mother.' Belinda was over-whelmed again, the whole situation being just too much for her.

Apparently, so I am told by the others, there was a loud cry, almost a scream. It was so loud that the whole group nearly jumped out of their skins. Then the cry intensified and it became louder and louder. Alf commented later that the room felt as if it were buzzing with a sort of activity he'd never experienced before. All this was going on and I was still by the camp fire watching these Indians feasting and talking. I was totally out of it. Pam described to me later, how, as the medicine man's chant intensified, more voices joined in. Belinda became hot and began to perspire heavily, so did Alf. Everyone began to feel hotter and hotter. Belinda cried uncontrollably as the chanting became more and more intense.

Then, as sharply and abruptly as it had started, it stopped. It was as if someone had pulled out the plug from the music centre. All the family agreed they were left with the greatest sense of peace. They felt relaxed and very hot. And me, well, I was still next to the camp fire – typical, I missed all the excitement!

Barry had been told by Jason, my guide, to start to bring me back as the trance state I'd been in had been very deep to allow the intensity of the healing to come through strongly. I began to hear Barry's voice, 'David. Come back, David.'

It took about five minutes, I was told, to bring me back and my reward was, of course, a large piece of milk chocolate to restore some energy. All the others were yawning and almost falling asleep looking at me – I was wide awake, buzzing with renewed energy. Everyone around me had been so relaxed by the ethereal forces, they just wanted to go to bed and sleep. I had been in the trance for over an hour and a half and it was almost 11-30pm. 'Time flies when you are having fun at an Indian barbecue, doesn't it?' I thought.

Simon and Belinda left for home which was only five minutes away. Pam and Alf said good night and went to bed. I wasn't tired, but Andrea and Barry were, so I complied and we climbed the stairs.

As we prepared for bed, Andrea remarked that she didn't know how she had stopped herself from breaking down with Belinda, but she had found the strength from somewhere. I was full of questions. As Andrea got into bed and put her head on the pillow, I was still talking, but she had gone to sleep – out like a light. But could I get to sleep? No chance! I kept going over the remarkable event in my mind, trying to piece things together. The atmosphere again danced around the room – despite my eyes being wide open.

I didn't know what exactly I'd done, but I do know that night something very special and of significance happened in the Wilsons' living room.

Simon and Belinda had previously had a sitting with me a few years before and found most of what I had said to be poignant and true. At that time, they had received useful information, but, unfortunately, it didn't reveal that children were on the horizon.

Just a couple of months after the fateful sitting at Barry's

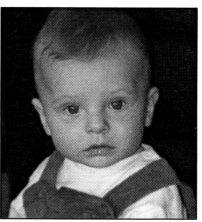

The young Spiritual Master, Matthew Gray, aged 18 months.

parents' house, we were all at the start of our holiday in France. The setting was the Loire Valley. We had hired a chateau for the first week and on the first night I approached Simon and told him he was going to be a father. He looked astounded. 'Yes, it's true,' he replied. Belinda had become pregnant not long after the trance healing with the Indian witchdoctor.

'To be honest,' Simon continued, 'we've been in shock ever since. We still can't believe it is going to happen for us. We can't thank you enough.'

'It's not me,' I emphasised. 'It's the Spirit World and the way in which the whole of creation works. There was a Spirit on the other side who just needed a little help from the higher powers that be, to enable him to take up Belinda's bodily offer of a vehicle to travel around the physical world again.'

'You mean he *had* been here before David?' Simon questioned.

'Oh yes, definitely. Some of my guides say that he is a much evolved soul who wishes to have another shot at life.'

'Amazing isn't it?' said Simon thoughtfully.

Some months after this holiday we travelled down to Barry's parents' home again and this time the spirits indicated again that they wished to come through and speak to Barry's family. We had enjoyed a lovely lunch in a very old country pub near Kelvedon. On our return Barry was given instructions, via a light trance communication with Jason, to build a cabinet in Pam's living room which would accommodate a human being and to obtain a red-coloured light bulb. This would enable the spirits to show themselves in a clearer manner. Not wanting to disappoint them, we did as we were told.

One broken lampshade later, the cabinet was finished, the red light switched on and I was left alone seated inside it. Immense energy was generated within the cabinet and I was soon with the North American Indians by their fire, having a barbecue.

I should explain how the cabinet is constructed. It has three sides and a roof. A chair is placed in the cabinet for the Medium to sit on. The red light provides illumination. The cabinet is a powerful way of enhancing spiritual communication. It helps to hold the energies and direct them. It almost intensifies them. The red light attracts Spirit and also helps individuals in the room to see any physical changes taking place on or around the Medium. I was introduced to this aid to communication in the development circle with Jim Roe and the team at Moor Lane Church, Preston. Under

Jim's guidance I learned a lot about trance Mediumship, physical Mediumship and cabinet work. Barry, also, was acquainted with this method. We both knew exactly what we were doing and we had no hesitation in using the cabinet. In addition, we knew that we would be well protected by the Spirit.

I must say at this point that it is not advisable for you to try this at home. So please heed my advice: it is not a Harry Potter make-believe situation; it's a very real situation and one that has to be conducted only by people who are experienced in these matters.

Throughout the sitting in Pam and Alf's living room, members of their family came through whom I had never met or known anything about, each time my voice apparently changing to their accent and timbre. Andrea commented later that she could see them queuing up behind me. At one point an Indian chief took over and it was possible to see the physical change and head-dress on me.

Each time, the members of the Wilson family on the other side congratulated Pam and the family about Belinda's pregnancy and re-assured them all would be well with the little chap. It was during this demonstration that it was confirmed that Matthew would be no ordinary child. He was himself a Spiritual Master.

The evidence arising during this demonstration from the cabinet was mind-blowing stuff. Alf had spoken to his mother and father and Pam to her mum. It was evident that Matthew would bring much to his loved ones here and also evidence and proof of where he had come from – the Spirit World.

Belinda takes up the extraordinary story now. This story gives hope to those who have lost children and those who want children desperately. It shows us that our children are Spirit, they come from Spirit and return to Spirit. They have the choice of whether to take a new life or to stay on the other side when they have crossed over. How wonderful that Nature re-creates life in this way. What seems to be a tragedy and a waste, thus becomes a source of joy. Our little ones live on and that's amazing.

The events leading up to the birth of Matthew Gray

Having suffered from Crohn's Disease since May 2000, I was beginning to think that I might never have children. Whenever I thought the time was right, the disease flared up, I became stressed and subsequently had to have two operations, which set me back further. It didn't help that I was getting older too (35).

Simon and I had often spoken about having children but is seemed that everyone around us was having all the luck except us. We had spoken to the family about this on a number of occasions. Barry, David and Andrea had been a part of some of these conversations. Everyone knew that we wanted children.

One weekend in March, 2005 when Barry, David and Andrea visited, my life was changed completely, for the better. We had been discussing family matters and following a meal that evening in a nearby restaurant, Pierre (one of David and Barry's Spirit Guides) visited us in the car park and informed Barry and David that my dad, Alf, and I were to receive some intensive healing that night, mine specifically for fertility.

Barry was told to go home and put on all the lights in the lounge and seat both of us on the sofa with our hands in our laps, feet on the floor and to close our eyes and relax. David sat to our right, with Barry by his side as 'the doorkeeper'. Andrea, Simon and my mum, Pam, were also in the room sitting at the other end. David then started to go into a trance. I recall Simon being asked at one point to come and kneel in front of David so that he could use some of Simon's energy as he too was getting very hot due to the activity that was happening.

Throughout the whole time, I experienced a lot of heat being generated in my body. I believe it was Pierre who said, towards the end, that we would feel very emotional and tired following the healing. We were told to open our eyes and the next thing I remember was talking about the experience and Andrea sitting by my side holding my hand as I burst into tears; I just didn't know what to expect next. I began talking about the possibility of having children and was re-assured that all would be well. I felt totally relaxed. Some time after the experience, I began to feel calmer in myself and my Crohn's Disease began to ease. I visited my consultant who announced that I was now in remission.

I didn't think any more of it and lived my life as normal until one afternoon in June, 2005 I got a very pleasant shock. It was the day prior to our going on a family holiday to France. We were to travel to my brother's home in Berkshire and stay the night before going on to Portsmouth the next morning. I was at home alone, getting together the last-minute bits and pieces, when suddenly I felt an unaccountable urge to do a pregnancy test. I had bought some tests previously and that afternoon I took the plunge. To my delight the result was positive. Simon came home and I was standing in the lounge doorway with the result in my hand. He was over the moon. I hurried to the phone to double check with the NHS Direct if it was okay for me to continue taking the tablets prescribed for Crohn's Disease, during pregnancy. We then picked up my parents and off we went.

During the car journey I answered a follow-up call from NHS Direct. This was rather cryptic as my parents were in the car and I didn't want them to know yet. I discovered later that my mum thought I was discussing IVF fertility treatment.

Whilst on holiday, I was careful not to say or do anything that would cause people to think I was pregnant. One day, Simon was approached by David who said, 'You've got something to tell us, haven't you?' Simon replied, 'You tell me.'

David said, 'There will be a baby in nine months.' Simon smiled and said, 'We won't be saying anything for a few months until we know all is O.K., so don't say anything to anyone else.'

David agreed not to discuss it further but mentioned that he already knew the sex of the child.

Eight weeks into the pregnancy, Simon and I told our parents and, following the 12-week-scan, the rest of the family was told. We also told everyone about how David already knew.

I recall David saying, during another conversation, that the baby would literally 'pop' out of my tummy into the world.

Matthew decided not to arrive on time and I was told by Barry and David that he would arrive within the next week. David was right about his 'popping' out of my tummy – he was born by Caesarean, in February, 2006, a very healthy 7lb. 6½oz. baby.

He is our little miracle and to this day we are grateful to our Friends in High Places *for their help.*

Matthew has grown into a very handsome boy and along the way has received healing from David, Barry and Andrea. From birth Matthew has suffered from a milk allergy. However, David told us that he would grow out of it before the age of two. Now, at 19 months, he has done so. We were also advised by David not to worry about his teeth. Matthew is advanced for his age, having almost a full set of them by 19 months. This message came a couple of days before we visited the paediatrician about Matthew's milk allergy. He too, remarked that Matthew was advanced with his teeth and should normally have had the amount of teeth he has by the age of 2½. This was likely to be the cause of Matthew's rejection of lumpy food. Along the way it has been great to have reassurance from David.

Matthew had a spiritual naming ceremony for his first birthday which was a lovely experience. We are glad that he is able to be brought up as part of a large family, of which we feel David and Andrea are very much a part.

Simon and I thank them greatly for all their support but it does give a new meaning to 'it takes two to make a baby' – in our case there were many more!!

Chapter 9

My mission

You know, when we lose a child – indeed anyone we love – the grief and pain we experience can be immense. I can't find the words to express what it must feel like. I suppose, after the initial loss, we have a tendency as human beings to reach out and grasp at anything, absolutely anything that can help us come to terms with the loss, pain and suffering that we are feeling. That pain is not something which comes and goes intermittently. It is constant.

Consulting a Medium is common in such a situation. However, I also believe that this is not a route for everyone. Why do I say this? Surely, anyone who has lost a child would be desperate to find a way to keep in touch? You would expect most people to attempt to do so. Well, the reality of the situation is that it isn't the view of some people and my next case will help you to understand why.

One Wednesday evening, we took our road show to Liverpool again with much success. A full house greeted me and happily, in return, many received a message from their loved ones on the other side of life. I had just finished a great link with a guy in the Spirit called George. He'd come through to his ex-wife, in the audience, to apologise. His words were that he'd "buggered off" with some-one else years ago and he shouldn't have, because he still loved his first wife. She had the audience in fits of laughter; her Liverpool humour, her colourful language in her replies to him and her fun-loving personality shone out. I couldn't carry on, I was laughing so much.

I decided enough was enough and was about to go into the interval when a youngish male began to link in with me. He was tall, very well built, very 'physical' looking. He must have worked out at the gym or had a physically strenuous job. He was a fine figure of a man, hair sandy brown, just brushed back. He seemed to me to be in his early twenties. I actually described him as having 'film star' looks. I even told the audience he could have been a professional model. He was smartly dressed and he stood confidently by my side.

Without any hesitation, he directed me to a table in the far corner of the room. If you have never visited the Taxi Club, I should tell you that it's a very large venue with lots of tables. People must feel pretty 'dropped-on' if a complete stranger looks directly at their table and starts to describe their loved one, giving the name and how that person crossed over.

As I started to communicate with those at the table in the corner, the whole atmosphere in the room changed. Everyone seemed to become involved emotionally. As the evidence streamed through there wasn't a dry eye in the house.

I haven't gone into much detail about this communication for reasons I'm sure you will understand shortly. The communication had become so strong and so emotional I decided to bring it to a close. I asked the young man to step back and then I left his loved ones at the table. I was aware that if I did not stop at that point, I would be emotionally drained myself.

At that time, I believed that that particular communication was one of the best links I'd had the privilege to be part of. The details were so accurate: the times, the dates, every part of it was strong and good.

Sitting in the dressing room in the interval, sipping my water, I thought to myself, that young lad is, without a doubt, a brilliant communicator. He had been so concerned about everything to do with his crossing and the people he had left behind, including his parents who, incidentally, were not seated in my audience at the time. I had literally blown myself away with this one. I said to myself, 'Well, David, you never had any doubts about the Spirit World and life after death and that link has just confirmed your belief.'

The second half of the demonstration in Liverpool was drawing to a close. I wished I could keep going through the night. I love it so much, I really do. But, reluctantly, I had to call it a day. At the end of the demonstration, the people who had been sitting at the table, indicated by the handsome young man in Spirit, came over to thank me. I could tell by their excitement and ease that the communication had impressed them. If it only provided them with relief for a short while, I'm sure it was worth it.

Time flies when you're having fun and just a week later I was getting myself ready to leave for my event in the sunny seaside town of Southport, not a million miles from where I live. I'd finished my meditation and was just about to leave when a familiar Spirit man came towards me. 'Hi, mate,' he said cheerfully. It was the same good-looking lad who had come through at Liverpool.

'Hi there,' I replied.

'I need to communicate again in Southport, mate,' he told me.

'O.K.,' I replied.

Then he gave me the names of some of the people who would be seated in the audience – if they had succeeded in gaining admission. The people in question had not reserved seats; they were coming along hoping to pay on the door. However, at some demonstrations we have had to turn away people who have not troubled to book and have come on 'spec'. This is because the attendance limit set by the Fire Certificate at a given venue has already been reached. At our demonstrations, when people book as parties, they do so under just one name but I never know who is coming as Brian deals with the list and I never see it. I explained this to the young man and asked him to direct me to his friends. The demonstration was to take place at the Royal Clifton Hotel. I was relieved when the young man left because I did not want to be disturbed by his presence while I was driving to Southport.

The preliminaries were over, the demonstration was under way and, as promised, the young man stepped forward. Again, he communicated strongly. His friends received him openly and happily again. The room was filled with tears of simultaneous sadness, joy and love for the young man. Before he left, he asked his girlfriend to ask his parents to attend a demonstration. He was desperate to communicate with them both. I could only imagine their pain at the loss of such a lovely young man. He obviously needed them to know he was well and although he had lost his body, his life wasn't over. He had crossed over quickly and suddenly and it seemed to be of great importance to him to contact his parents.

Again, at the end of Southport's demonstration, the young man's friends and girlfriend came to thank me. They each in turn put their name on my one-to-one sitting list, thanked me again and left. The one-to-one sittings are usually very successful. Most of the time, the evidence for life after death is overwhelming.

At this point, I must apologise for the brief way in which I am dealing with this episode, but I am sure you will understand as we go on. My sitting lists are long and my diary is always full with church services, private demonstrations, charity events and, of course, one-to-one sittings. The lists are made up of people's names and telephone numbers only and when slots are available, they are contacted.

After a short-notice cancellation, I had gone down my list phoning people to fill the slot. Out of the 90 numbers I called, only one answered and it was this young man's girlfriend. She immediately took the slot and received an excellent communication, after which she was filled with joy. I could tell that for certain. At the end, she commented that it had been as if her boyfriend had been sitting in the same room, which was a lovely compliment to me and the Spirit World, who make all this possible.

What emerged from her conversation was that her boyfriend's parents were in a terrible state; their pain was immense after this tragic loss. She asked me if she could bring them along to see me. Rarely do I see people immediately, but it was evident to me that they needed help. If my communicating for them would give them even some minor relief from their grief, then I would do my best. I agreed on a date with her. Although she hadn't yet spoken to them about me, she would talk to them, tell them about what had happened in Liverpool and Southport and would bring them along as arranged.

She told me that the communication had helped her so much she felt a weight had been lifted from her shoulders and she felt able to move on. She said she would bring the young man's parents, but not be a part of their sitting herself.

The sitting soon came around and, as usual, I spent the hour before in meditation. I felt relaxed and open to the Afterworld; everything was in place so there was no reason for me not to have a fantastic link and communication for the young man's parents.

The door bell rang and I received them in the usual way, talking and trying to put them at their ease. The lad's mother seemed open to the idea of communication from her son, but her husband was obviously not comfortable.

Their son tried to give evidence; he was clearly anxious to speak to his parents. I could see him plainly in the Afterworld. Everything I said to his father was received with a negative response and eventually a closed response until he seemed totally to lose patience. After 15 minutes he stood up, exclaimed he'd had enough and wished to leave. His wife looked distraught, all her hopes of being in touch with her son had been dashed in that split second.

I can admit to you all, right now, that after this particular sitting, with the most excellent strength of communication that had led up to it, I felt flat and negative. I likened it to being on a rollercoaster ride – a high point followed by a low. At this juncture, I contemplated giving up my Mediumship completely. This is the only time – and I stress this honestly – the only time I have considered this. Not for one moment, though, do I believe that the Spirit World would have allowed this to happen.

The young man's parents left; the manner of their leaving and the disappointment I felt, due to the persistent barrage of negativity on the part of the young man's father, made it impossible for me to communicate properly. The father's lack of belief and strength of character, emanating that disbelief, affected me in the most human way. I believe that the pain of their loss was so great, it acted as a barrier to any help that I, as a Medium, could have given them.

To this day, I think about them often and still wish them peace in their hearts.

After my unhappy experience with this couple, I approached Jason my guide. I wanted to know why this had happened to me

– if I had been tested in some way. I was desperate. Jason's answer was that,

'in this life, everyone has the free-will and freedom of choice. Some choose to seek comfort by gaining evidence of the spiritual existence of their loved ones and some do not. No human being should be forced to communicate with their loved ones. If they choose not to, it must be so. Their grief must be respected by all and controlled by none. To attempt to control someone else's grief is to take away their freedom of emotion. Some grieve for ever, never finding the peace they need to bring their life back to what it was. Some grieve for a short time and then find the strength to put their sorrow behind them and move on. Each individual is unique. No-one should be cajoled, badgered or talked into attempting to communicate with their loved one through the Spiritual Masters.'

Jason was right, God bless him. Tears rolled down my cheeks as I brushed my teeth in the bathroom. Well, if you're going to wear a smile through a bad patch, then it's got to be a bright one.

My journey to Leigh Spiritualist Church, Lancashire seemed to take for ever that night, the traffic was so heavy. Then, to top it all, I had terrible problems in parking. All the way down to Leigh my mind had been going over the above events and then to Jason's advice. I decided I had to put it all behind me if the demonstration at Leigh Church were going to be successful. So, I imagined an open drawer, put all the negatives in it and closed it. I had to do that because it would have been unfair of me to stand in front of the congregation and lead the demonstration if I had not been in the correct frame of mind.

The service at Leigh was outstanding. Many communicators from the Afterworld came forward, directing me to their loved ones in the audience. The strength of evidence was great too. As I look back on the service, I feel it was almost as if the Spirit World were saying: 'Hey David, sometimes you are going to have unsuccessful sittings, but you have to overcome them. So look forward to giving positive messages to those who are receptive and continue on the path chosen for you to help others.'

After I'd finished the demonstration, I was asked to step down from the rostrum as members of the church committee were about to prepare for a healing session. I began to make my way through the crowds of people. Someone asked for quietness and silence fell over the church. A lady in her early 40s began to wave at me from the other side of the room. Despite the plea for quietness, she continued to beckon me. As I made my way across the hall, I could see she was sitting with an older lady and a young girl.

'Hello, how are you,' I whispered, conscious of the need for quietness. The lady who had beckoned me looked so sad.

'I'm desperate,' she exclaimed. Her companions merely stared at me. The young girl seemed blank and numb with grief and pain. 'Was there anyone for me at all, David?' asked the lady in her 40s.

'Well, during the service there wasn't,' I said quietly and then, after a pause, I added, 'but I have a young male joining me; he is your son, isn't he love? He is only in his teens – 17/18 years, that's all. He tells me he crossed into the Spirit in a vehicle accident.'

The boy then gave me his name, the name of his sister, his mother and his grandmother. I have never heard such an outpouring of grief in my life. Everyone stopped and looked. They all began to hug each other as their loved one told them, in detail, what had happened. He told them about a birthday due to occur during the next few days. They were absolutely overjoyed. He told them he was well in the other world. I was so involved in the communication that the experience with the couple, which had upset me so much, began to recede from my mind. This mother's thanks were all I needed to convince me that I should carry on my work as a Spirit Medium.

I subsequently tried to contact this family at Leigh, to find out whether the message they received helped them. The committee at the church tried too, as the family was recognised as frequently attending the church but, since the message, they have not been seen. Maybe they got what they needed to help them move on with their lives. One day, I hope to see them again, just to thank them and let them know they are the reason I continued with my Mediumship.

As I said my good-byes in the church hallway, a voice came into my head, 'Now who was going to give up then?'

I glanced to my side; it was Jason, my wonderful guide.

'Was it you by any chance?' he continued.

'No, not me,' I replied in my head voice. 'You must have the wrong Medium.'

He winked his eye and smiled.

Whether people believe that I talk to their loved ones or they don't, whether they dismiss me or whatever, I feel that it is a privilege to have my gift, to work for the Spirit World and ultimately the Creator, God. Oh yes, it is He and He alone who has given me this gift to help others on Earth.

Being a Spirit Medium is one of the most difficult vocations I know of. It's a lonely life at times and the responsibility to people and their needs is limitless. In addition, much of your life is spent wondering if people are thinking you're crazy or something. Further, there is a need to find time for sorting out any troublesome people. Sadly, everyone, there are some misguided people out there who make some awful derogatory comments about you and your supposed life and yet, the stark truth is they don't know the first thing about you, your life, or Mediumship. Some profess their expertise, without ever volunteering any proof of how they could possibly make such assumptions. We are expected to accept, at face value, that they, the detractors, are as 'savvy' as they claim.

Once, when I got home from a Stockport event, I turned on the TV and Princes William and Harry were being interviewed. Explaining that they found it difficult to come to terms with how people *perceive* them, William said it's really hard when people, with pre-conceived ideas, talk to them and are then surprised that the Princes are different from their unrealistic expectations. All of us are who we are – not what someone, who may have never met us, thinks we are. I agreed with William when he said, 'If you want to know something about me, then ask, don't just build up a picture from what someone else says.' I endorse that argument.

I have included the above in my book to enable me to make the following mission statement:

If ever I subject anyone to the lies and deceit that I, or my persona, have been subject to and I do that knowingly, then I will give up Mediumship, because the essence of being a Medium is <u>truth</u>, on all levels.

Chapter 10

Marie, Vivienne and Vera

Time flies when you're having fun, so every Thursday evening that I have free in my schedule I take myself off to the Purple Light Spiritualist Church at Chorley. I had no clue who would be demonstrating that night, but it really wouldn't have mattered whoever it would be as each Medium brings something new to the rostrum, something individual. I believe each person teaches you something.

So, that afternoon I'd called into Wigan to pick up a shirt I had ordered some weeks before. Just as I was walking around Debenhams, my phone rang, which is in itself rather unusual because I can rarely get a signal in that store. It was my good friend June from Purple Light.

'David, are you free this evening, love, only I've had a cancellation for tonight at church. Could you take it for me?'

'Of course, yes, I'll do that June – no problem.'

I'd just got my words out and my phone cut off. Daft signal – drives me mad!

As I arrived that evening, I could see the church was packed as usual, the congregation was buzzing. It's a lovely experience there as everyone is so nice and friendly. The service ran as usual – prayers and hymns and then a philosophy. I never know what I am going to be talking about prior to the philosophy statement; I am just guided by one of the team on the other side.

As I stood up to speak I was advised that I would be talking about being ordinary, just being yourself, a statement, which I am sure my wife would comment, 'Him ordinary? Never!' I then burst out laughing.

I decided to tell the story of a one-to-one sitting I had attended. Yes, I can conduct Mediumship myself, I know, but I am only human, really I am. So, when it comes to one-to-one sittings, I have the same curiosity and need as you, although I don't go for many readings these days. I suppose this is because I am well known, and as my first book tells my story with much personal detail, it would be quite easy for someone to give evidence based on the information given in my book. So, when another Medium is recommended to me, adopting an alias and trying hard not to reveal my identity, I'll go for a private reading.

So my philosophy began and went something like this:

I am *ordinary* by self admission. There is nothing I like more than reading for a total stranger and bringing through lots of evidence for them from the other side. The more I do this for others, the more I seek this for me. I love the idea of someone communicating for me – maybe with my dad in the Spirit World.

A lady I know from Liverpool, called Marie, had been to see a Medium in Clwyd, North Wales. She described him as being brilliant. She went on and on, until I became convinced. Yes, he was sold to me, hook, line and sinker. But, I should have known that Marie isn't the greatest judge of character – she has given me permission to say this – and the confirmation of this is apparent with the six divorces under her belt! Oh yes, Marie is a true and eternal psychic junkie. I have read for her twice, but I've told her no more readings, it's unfair, as I know her too well. She trips off for readings maybe twice a week – though, sometimes, nearing Christmas, three or four times.

Unfortunately, I had to leave the Welsh medium's name out. However, for my philosophy I had called him Sid, the psychotic psychic!

I collected Marie from the city centre and we made our way through the Mersey tunnel heading towards Chester and North Wales. The only problem with my friend Marie is that if you're in her company or share a journey with her, she tries to pump you for a reading and on this particular occasion she was getting nowhere at all. She must have asked me 50 times in 50 different ways, what did I think about Steve? Could I get anything from the name

Steve? 'NO. I'm closed right now,' I repeated. 'Anyway, what's the point in me telling you if you're going to pay £25 to Sid? If I tell you, you will have wasted your time and your money.' For the rest of the journey she talked about gardening and nearly sent me into a coma!

It wasn't long before we were in Clwyd and the beautiful rolling countryside fell away into the distance. Marie guided me down a long, winding road. Even in daylight it felt a little creepy; one of those lanes you wouldn't like your car to break down on.

'There's the house, David,' said Marie, pointing as she spoke.

'Pull over onto that verge; it was all right to park there last time.'

The house was huge. I'd never seen a front door so big. Wisteria covered most of the house. I joked with Marie that it reminded me of a scene out of the *Rocky Horror Show*. As we stepped out of the car Marie said, 'Let's do the time warp again,' accompanying it with the actions.

I was beginning to get a little apprehensive as we walked up the drive towards the front door. The bell played the *1812 Overture*. I am not that great at recognising musical pieces, but I had to play an extract from that for a piano exam some years ago.

Two minutes later there was no answer, so I rang again. I just turned to Marie and said, 'You have booked Marie, haven't you?'

'Yes,' she replied. 'I've got the card in my bag.'

She began to root in her hand bag. As she did, the front door opened revealing a very tall gentleman, his hair quiffed at the front. His hair seemed too big for his little head, bless him.

'There's no need to press twice,' he snapped. 'I heard you the first time. Besides, you'll waste my batteries.'

There was no 'Hello, I'm Sid, nice to see you.' I could tell that this whole episode was going to be hard work, very hard work indeed.

'Sorry,' Marie said timidly.

I didn't apologise. Maybe I should have, thinking back.

'Well, no matter, you had better come in,' he snapped. He moved aside and we walked into the hall. He shut the door, turned and instructed, 'Can you keep to the plastic runner please, only it's a new carpet.'

I don't believe this, I thought. Then he took out a hanky and wiped the door knob. This had to be a joke. Marie was unaffected but I was already worked up. I know it was not very spiritual of me. He was a total nutter in my opinion.

Sticking to the plastic carpet protector I could see the house was immaculate – every plug socket shone. I felt like the Tin Man in *The Wizard of Oz*, walking next to Dorothy when they had to keep to the yellow brick road. I found myself watching every step. I felt very uncomfortable.

He led us to a room just off to the left at the back of the hall and we both sat in silence, like schoolchildren summoned by the headmaster.

'I'll just be a moment,' he announced. Then he asked me to join him in the room on the opposite side of the hallway. As I entered he told me to be seated. You know, at this point I trembled, I was actually becoming frightened of him.

'I am now going to take out my crystal ball,' he said in a very drawn-out Welsh accent. 'It's in the box,' he added.

'Oh,' I said quietly.

To my complete surprise, he lifted out a glass ball the size of a football and placed it on a stand already on the desktop between us.

'That's a big one,' I joked to try to lighten the atmosphere, but in my mind I was thinking I could strangle Marie right now.

'I've never seen one so big,' I said again, my tummy wobbling as I began to laugh.

My joke went down like a lead balloon.

'Now place both your hands on the ball please,' he said seriously.

The heat from my hands could have warmed a house. My palms felt on fire. Each word he spoke was now making me laugh inside, my stomach shaking. He must have detected this. I lifted my hands from the ball and there were two clear hand prints left on the glass – my hands had obviously perspired with the heat coming from them.

'Now look what you have done, you mucky pup, you've left your paw prints on my ball. I don't know!' he snapped, taking his hanky out and removing the offending marks immediately. At this point, the congregation at Purple Light burst out laughing so loudly you could have heard them on the other side of Chorley – or even in Clwyd. 'A real belly laugh is good for you,' I exclaimed to the congregation.

Anyone reading this would think this can't be true – trust me. This is all God's honest. I was now beginning to seethe; I just couldn't believe he was being so fussy. Steam was coming out of my nose and ears. I was turning into the original Welsh dragon.

Again the laughter was topped up by my comments. Next he began to moan and groan, 'I see a dog, friend,' he said. 'Can you take a dog in the Spirit World please? It's drawing close to you,' he added.

'Which one? I have several dogs in the Spirit World,' I replied, still wondering why I was there and trying now desperately not to show my annoyance.

'No, not several dogs you fool, there's only one here, on the left.'

'Yes, but I still don't …' I hadn't got my words out and Sid snapped back, 'It's only got one *ear* on the left you fool, that's the evidence, it's only one ear.' He was seeing red. The congregation was in fits of laughter.

What was really rude of me though, and I do regret it to this day, was, as he lost his temper, I burst out laughing in his face. I was hysterical. I do genuinely regret that.

Very abruptly, without a smile Sid retorted, 'It's a sort of an Irish wolfhound, but it has very short legs.'

That was it. Two tears popped out of my eyes as though from a water pistol; they splattered on the desk. I was rolling with laughter. The members of the congregation at Purple Light were beside themselves with mirth.

I was totally out of control in front of Sid. He stood up and ordered me out of his house. I was relieved to be honest; the whole sitting from the start had been a complete embarrassment. As I exited the front door, it slammed behind me. My thoughts could only go to Marie: I did hope she wouldn't suffer due to my insensitive lack of manners. I sat in my car waiting for Marie, the tears flowing down my face freely. My chuckle-muscles ached.

Sincerely, I have never laughed as much in all my life – Chorley congregation hadn't either.

Then I suddenly thought of Marie. I'd given her my £25 as she was paying for us both – 'Bet he'll charge,' I thought, even though I was ejected after ten minutes. Mind you, £25 for a really good laugh was well worth every penny.

Marie was walking towards the car. As she climbed in she exclaimed, 'God, he was in a foul mood. Did you have a good reading, David?'

'No, I didn't,' I said. 'Anyway, how did you get on?' I asked inquisitively.

'Great. He told me loads about Steve. Yes, really good.' Then, in all seriousness, Marie said, 'He said he had an Irish wolfhound with short legs and one ear. I couldn't take it. He said it was probably a Spirit guide. Anyway, I paid for the two of us.'

I just burst out laughing again and so did my congregation.

Maybe the moral to this story, I continued, is don't build up your expectations too much. After all, Mediums are only human beings and we shouldn't judge a Medium by someone else's experiences, because everyone's experience will be different.

It had been a great illustration. Now it was time for my demonstration of clairvoyance. During that, I managed to link with eight people. Each of the messages was acknowledged and accepted as accurate. Eventually, the demonstration was over and Rick, the chairman, called me to time – everyone cheered and clapped. It was a good response from the Purple Light audience. I'd gone down well, thank God, and my guides were brilliant. I'm nothing without them.

After the service, there is an interval where you can have tea or coffee and a biscuit and, of course, a chat. Then there's an "open circle". This is the part of the evening where anyone can stand up and give a message to anyone else. I decided to stay around and join in with the circle, even though I'd taken the service. After collecting a cup of coffee, I decided to steal a moment and step outside to cool off. It was really warm in the church that night, I was suffocating. I stood outside sipping coffee and acknowledging people as they left, as not everyone stays behind for the circle. A voice from behind me said, 'David.' I turned around a little startled.

'Hi David, how are you?'

'O.K., I answered,' not having a clue who the lady was in front of me. Yet deep inside, the way she had addressed me it felt as though I should have known her. The lady had a lovely mane of strawberry blonde, curly hair. Standing side-by-side with her was an older lady.

'You don't remember me do you, David?' she asked.

'No,' I answered, 'but I've a memory like a sieve.' It was a spur of the moment explanation, as I didn't want to seem ill-mannered. She continued, 'Well David, I was at Purple Light all those years ago. I was sat next to you when the Medium, who was demonstrating that night, pointed to you and said you were going to be on the stage doing Mediumship demonstrations and your name would be up in lights. You were shocked, I could tell from the look on your face.'

'Yes,' I replied, 'very shocked.' I must be honest, that's one evening I have never forgotten. The Medium astounded me with her revelations and each one, I must say, has come true.

The lady then said, 'Well, sometime later David I came to Purple Light Spiritualist Church and I won two tickets to see your demonstration at East Ward Conservative Club, Chorley. There, I was shocked when I received a message from you saying I was waiting to conceive a baby, the child would be fine and healthy and it was on its way soon. I thought to myself, "Well, David, you got that one wrong," for nothing at all was further from my mind. I was 40 and settled in everything I was doing – my job, my life and no plans. So I said no to what you said, David.'

'Well I'm really sorry about that,' I replied. I genuinely thought she was upset with me.

'Hold your hand out, David,' she said sternly.

Oh God, she's going to slap my wrists, I thought. Then, from its hiding place behind the pair of them, she popped a small child's car seat into my hand.

'You said she was coming and here she is – meet Harriet. She was born just 12 months later. Well, who is responsible for that one then?' The ladies burst out laughing. 'However, I wouldn't be without her now. Yes, you did say she would change our lives, and yes, she has – for the better.' She looked down at the little bundle

Harriet, the surprise package for her mother Vivienne Woods.

of joy and, dotingly, she said softly, 'Haven't you? You have changed our lives for the better?' We all looked down at the little angel.

'Suits you that,' the older lady chipped in.

'No fear,' I replied and, at that point, I handed little baby Harriet back to her mother, just in case the baby-making thing was contagious!

'Good luck with her. A little gift from the Spirit World, that's what she is. Bless you all.' Smiling I walked back inside, handed in my mug and sat down in the circle.

Vivienne's Story

I have had an interest in Spiritualism since my teenage years, having been introduced via a friend to the shows and books of Doris Stokes. There was never really anything significant about my journey. When I lost my father I became more interested and wanted 'proof' and started going to Spiritualist Church meetings, which I found to be very friendly and uplifting.

I eventually made contact with my father through the Church and a private sitting, at which I was satisfied with the results.

I had good faith in a Medium, Vera Higginson. However, at Church I didn't really get any messages until my involvement with David Traynor. I won two tickets to go and see David – I hadn't a clue who David Traynor was, or whether he would be any good. I just saw it as being an enjoyable evening out with my friends, made all the better for being in a club!

When David came onto the stage I recognised his face from Church, but I cannot recall ever having received a message off him previously. He had a message for me and spoke to me about my family and holidays. My sister was by my side and she took most of the message. He then spoke to me about a child that was going to be conceived to me. Having stated at 40 years of age children were not for me, I told him he was wrong. He laughed and said, 'Well actually you will see within two months and it's a little girl, she is here and she is waiting to come to you.' My sister got excited. I just thought – 'Well, he's no good is he?'

I came out later and kept thinking about that message. In July my pregnancy was confirmed and Harriet Georgia, my little girl, was born in March. I then started to say as I went to Church, 'David Traynor was there, you know, my Medium who told me about my child.' My friends and family became aware of who 'my Medium' was. I attended the Purple Light Church again in June of this year as I was aware that 'my Medium' was the guest and I brought along a friend who was new to the Church – not a sceptic, but also not really a believer and had certainly never seen David Traynor. For the last reading he came to me and he told me at the beginning about how I would help people in a similar situation to me in the future – which I had to take. I didn't completely understand.

He told me also about my lost child – a little boy – and the facts that he gave were not only correct but were completely mind-blowing. I sat and listened in amazement as he talked and talked about my life and at that moment all my concerns that I ever had, or little doubts, drifted. He was absolutely amazing. Many in the congregation were crying, including my friend. She also knew that what he was telling me was absolutely perfect.

What I found bizarre, was that week leading to my visit to the church I had been feeling guilty about my Spirit Child. I thought to myself that I had moved on, had my perfect little girl and have never forgotten about my Spirit Child, but did not do anything to celebrate him e.g. plant a tree, name him. I was thinking about that a lot and how I could rectify that.

After the show David asked that if anyone was pleased with their message, could it be placed on his website as he has a guest book – a way of thanking him and assisting others. I came away thinking that is the least I can do for him and I wrote my message the following morning. What better tribute can I give to my Spirit Child, I have asked myself – absolutely none.

It is only now that I look upon the latest message and think how Spiritualism has helped me to cope with my loss and grief and look at it positively. Of course, now it makes sense that 'I will one day help others' as I am sure that if any person reading my message, having been through what I have, there will be a connection and I hope that they receive hope, peace and contact from their loved one and grow from my experience, as I have most certainly done, thanks to the world of spirit.

Vivienne Woods

June gathered us all together. The circle was really popular and tonight it was huge. June announced that once she opened the circle, everyone would have to stay within its confines; no-one could leave until the end. Apart from other considerations, these guidelines help you to concentrate and maintain discipline. If people are walking in and out, for the toilet or any other reason, it can be very distracting.

June opened the circle up with a prayer asking the guides to protect our circle. Then she gave a brief explanation of how the circle worked and then stated that if anyone had a message they were to stand up and give the message to the person for whom it was intended. My attention was drawn to a smaller lady over to my right-hand side. She had red/brown, bobbed hair. She was very smartly dressed and smiled pleasantly as I looked at her; it was almost as though she knew I was going to her. There was a strong sense which drew me towards this lovely lady. As I watched, I could see a good-looking younger male in his early 20s, I could feel him pressing me and willing me to speak to the lady.

So, I stood up and greeted her with a big smile.

'Hello, can I speak with you please?' I asked politely.

'Yes of course,' she replied.

'I have a younger gentleman joining me now. He only looks 21 or 22 years of age, quite good looking, he has long shaggy hair. He makes me feel he crossed over in a motor vehicle accident. He also makes me want to call you mum, so I know you are his mum. He gives me the name of Paul. Do you understand, please?' I said confidently.

The lady smiled pleasantly, 'Yes, that's lovely, it's my son, my lovely son, and you've said his name, Paul, and yes, he did cross over in a road accident, that's all true my dear,' she confirmed calmly.

What I found so odd was the lovely lady's reaction. She was so calm, almost as if she didn't need me to tell her that Paul's spirit had survived the accident, even if his physical body had not.

Vera and Philip Higginson's son, Paul, from a painting in their home.

'Now he is showing me a lovely house near a motorway. This house is very near where the accident takes place, he tells me. He takes me back to the motorway. I believe he is trying to tell me that the road, which he is showing me, is the place where the accident happened.'

'That's true, love,' the lady said smiling.

I still couldn't get over the lady and her smile; the joy just radiated from her.

'He takes me to a cottage-style house.'

'Yes, that's mine love, that's where I live,' she replied.

'He is telling me he loves you so much.'

'I love him too,' she replied genuinely.

'He is giving me links to Judaism and Jewish connections.'

'Yes, that's my husband's side of the family, love, they are Jewish.'

'He gives me the name Phil.'

'Yes, that's my husband's name, my dear,' she confirmed.

'He also gives me the name, Vera.'

'Yes, that's me. I'm Vera.'

'Oh, nice to meet you, Vera,' I said, totally at ease in her presence.

'Paul gives me healing for you both. One of you had a fall and the other has been ill.'

'Correct,' she said.

'He is talking about you stepping back a little in your occupation.'

'Yes, I understand, dear.'

'He tells me you have too heavy a work schedule. Now he takes me to the month of March. Can you understand please?' I asked.

'Yes, his anniversary is March.'

'He is with you all the time, my love.'

'I know he is, trust me when I say I know,' she replied.

'He tells me you can do this, you have the gift also. Do you understand?' I asked. 'You too are a Medium?'

'Oh yes love, I've been a professional Medium for over 30 years, on and off the platform. I've seen them come and go, lovey,' she said smiling. 'But I've stepped back a little in my commitments. I've had a bit of a difficult time with my health, as you quite rightly said. You can't help anyone if you're not keeping good health yourself, can you? So, I've decided to take it easy, ... besides, we oldies have got to make way for you up-and-coming young Mediums,' she added. I thought that was a remarkably unselfish comment to make. I felt it was completely genuine and, I have to say, very spiritual of this lady to feel the way she did.

I ended my reading by leaving her son's love with her, but I followed that by saying, 'But you know that anyway.'

'I do, love,' Vera replied. 'But I am going to thank you for bringing him through. May I buy one of your books? I should like to read it.'

And that's how I met the renowned Spirit Medium, Vera Higginson. Later, people told me she was very well known. I was told she was a very reputable Medium. Since then I've had the pleasure of watching three of Vera's demonstrations, each of them a brilliant testimony to her life's work as a Medium.

Vera Higginson

My son Paul had trained to be a chef and then, in July 1987, he decided he wanted to go to America. We were very proud because he wanted to work at a Jewish Summer Camp (the Eisner Camp) in Massachusetts. The work was very poorly paid, but Paul was very keen to do it – and he did. When he returned in the October, he brought back with him a copy of a painting by famous American artist Norman Rockwell entitled 'Marriage Licence', his belated wedding present to us both. He also brought, for Philip whose ancestors were Jewish, a beautiful Jewish cup, which remains a treasured possession.

He enrolled at Preston College to study psychology and, because of poor public transport services, we bought him a moped. On November 2nd, he left early to avoid the rush hour traffic. At 8-45 a.m. I knew he had passed over, but when the police officers arrived at 9-30 a.m. to give me the news, I broke down completely. Only if you have lost a child can you know the utter devastation I felt.

Even though I am a Medium, with a lifetime spent working with Spirit, my loss is no less devastating; I am a human being, a mother. Only a parent who has lost a child can know the deep sense of loss and desolation this brings. The manner of Paul's passing only compounded my 'loss'. I knew that he was alive and well, but that lack of his physical presence was difficult to deal with. I gave up my work for several months until, one day, I sat sorrowfully in the dining room, unable to describe my feeling of deep despair and emptiness, my life seemingly at an end, questioning life's purpose and feeling there is no point in staying here.

Suddenly, the room was filled with a blinding light, so bright I had to shield my eyes. A tall figure in a shimmering white 'gown' stood before me, glorious in his light. This must have been an angel, but he had no wings. Bathed in his light, I felt a peace envelope me. He smiled, held out his hand and took hold of mine, saying gently, 'Do you not see how selfish you are? You have a husband and a daughter who need and love you – and you have much work to do, come and we will show you the way'. He then pulled me firmly but gently from my chair and then he faded away and with him, the light. I stood there for what seemed an age and an unexplained joy filled my heart, my whole being, as if I would burst wide open. My life had begun again.

Two days later, I took up the reins and gave my first sittings, I was very quickly busier than ever with my work for Spirit; it is an honour and a privilege which I cherish.

Paul often assists in my sittings and, as he has said of himself, 'I am more alive than you are'.

Vera M. Higginson

After I'd finished speaking to Vera I was joined by a younger lady of the Afterworld and she guided me to a young lady who was seated on the other side of the room. She had a lovely round, smiling face, stunningly pretty eyes and she sat with her friend, staring motionless into space. It seemed like she didn't have a clue what was going on in the circle. She seemed so empty. As I walked towards her I smiled and said, 'Can I come to you please?'

She must have been day-dreaming because she nearly jumped

out of her skin. 'Yes,' she smiled, putting her hand to her chest. 'Please do.'

'I have a lady joining me from the Afterworld. She tells me she is your mum and she had a cancer condition before she crossed over.' The girl just looked up at me and burst into tears.

'I think I can safely say, that's a yes,' I said quietly. The girl nodded. She was so overcome by it all.

'Now your mum is congratulating you on your engagement and your wedding is very soon; I am talking weeks away.'

'Yes. I can't believe it, that's all true,' she said. All of a sudden her tears of emotion turned into tears of joy.

'Oh, you've been for a final wedding dress fitting just recently and she tells me your dress is absolutely lovely. She says it's off the shoulders, plain but very elegant. Correct?' I enquired.

'Yes, that is right,' the girl replied, almost in shock.

'Who is Steven? Oh, I shouldn't ask, I'll tell you. Steven is giving you away, that's what your mum is saying.'

'He is,' she replied, now shaking her head in disbelief.

'Ah, now she tells me that the bridesmaids are in sky blue, again plain, but elegant ... and a mutual friend, of you and your mum, is making them.'

At this point the girl broke down again.

'I'm joined by your mum's mum, that's your grandmother. She said if she had been here she'd have made all the dresses, including yours, and made the cake and iced it. She was good like that.'

'I passed that comment only the other day to my friend,' the girl remarked. Her friend, sitting beside her, took hold of her hand saying, 'Yes, she did say that to me.'

'Now your fiancé, he must be called David, because your mum is telling me she likes David, unless she means she likes me,' I joked, to break the tension caused by the accuracy of the reading.

'Yes, he is called David,' she confirmed.

'Your mum tells me the last lad you were engaged to let you down ever so badly.'

'Yes, he did,' she answered, now very emotional again.

'She's taking me to Scotland for links. Do you understand?'

'Yes I do.'

'Edinburgh?'

'Correct.'

'Your mum says your dad let you down badly, after she had crossed over to the Spirit World. He sort of drifted away and now he has his own life with someone else. This has left you and Steven very disappointed and you feel you have no-one but each other. But listen, your mum says to me she will always come through to you if you go to any Medium. She'll always speak and communicate. She has never left your side, ever. She says she has been at all your pre-wedding arrangement meetings and she will not be missing a single moment of the day. She keeps telling me to tell you she loves you very much. You know what? I can sympathise with you. My sister-in-law crossed over at the age of 38. She left four children and I always say to them, 'You know, your mum left the greatest gift of all, she left us each other.' The same applies to you and Steven: you, too, have each other. How wonderful is that? How lovely to know that the most important day of your life is coming up and she'll be there watching everything, as all proud mums do at their daughter's wedding. My advice to you, sweetheart, is to make a mental note of everything that happens throughout your wedding day, all the details. If there's any funny moment, any little hiccup, then when you sit in front of a Medium again your mum will be able to give you the details of what happened. What will that tell you then?'

The girl looked puzzled, 'What do you mean?'

'Simply, what will it tell you if your mum comes through a Medium and gives very strong details about your wedding?'

The girl looked at me. I could see my question had clicked in her head. 'That she's been there watching,' she replied, again tearful.

'Correct,' I smiled. 'Now, have a lovely wedding and congratulations from me too.'

'Thank you so much,' the girl replied through her tears. I turned around and wiped a tear from my eye – well, I can get emotional too you know. I think I'd be right in saying I'm a big softie at heart.

June walked over, just like a mother hen. 'Are you bringing the proof to people, love?' she asked.

'Yes, I am,' I replied.

'Great. Keep up the good work, love,' she smiled and walked away. Such a spiritual lady, I thought, really true and genuine and ever so nice with it. Spirits are truly lucky to have her working for them.

I know my bridge isn't a one-way bridge. I have parents in the Afterworld who want to speak to their children here in the physical world as well. My bridge is for all angels to cross; I'm just the troll in the middle!

The circle came to an end and prayers were offered to the guides and inspirers and indeed our loved ones for working with us. As I got into my car a person, with a familiar face, tapped on my window. It was the lovely girl that I gave the message to. I wound down the window.

'Thanks so much. That's the icing on the cake for me,' she said. We both started to laugh.

'That's apt,' I replied. She began to walk up the road. As I was about to wind up my window, another lady who was standing nearby came up to my car and said, 'I just couldn't help listening, David, when you gave that message to that young girl. How lovely that was, to put her mind at ease. Keep up the good work dear, it's so appreciated and so necessary. 'Bye now.' She walked away. It was nice to hear. I am not a glory hunter, but a 'thank you' goes a long, long way. As I drove home, I thanked my guides and told them that they had done so much good in such a small space of time. Their good is essential to the Earth.

Chapter 11

Colin

Do you know, in these sittings not everything pings into place? Some connections are more difficult than others. Sometimes, in fact, the connection starts out weak and almost non-existent, then it turns into something quite the opposite – strong and almost physical. This is such a difficult occurrence and for this I have no explanation. I can only imagine that I am not tuned in and open enough or the particular Spirit is finding me difficult to link with. The following story illustrates what happens if you stick with a link that in the beginning you believe to be a non-starter.

I've been desperate to lose weight. For ages now, I've felt uncomfortable. When your waist-line expands from a size 32 to 38 or sometimes larger – well, it's no joke. Plus, I'm a binge eater. Often, I'll have my evening meal far too late and then I'll eat either chocolate, nuts or crisps. I need to sort out *my* 'battle of the bulge'. I joined a gym two years ago. I'm still a member, but guess what? I've not been for over a year. I must change my life-style; if I don't, one day I'll expand so much – I'll never get back to how I was.

Well, I'd been in Altrincham and on my way out from my venue a lady came over to me and said, 'Hey David, you are far podgier in life than on your photo.'

She laughed and I retorted, 'They wouldn't put my body on the front cover of the book – they said if they did, it would have to be an annual!'

The girl, who wasn't overly slim herself, laughed and said, 'bye.'

Something was triggered in my brain and, two days later, I was dieting with all the determination that I could muster so I should become thin – salads and more salads. I felt like Bugs Bunny! I was demonstrating in Widnes at the Hillcrest Hotel. I'd had lunch and a light dinner before leaving. As I started to demonstrate, my energy wasn't at all right. I had great links, great evidence, but it wasn't like it had been when I had demonstrated before I was dieting. I thought I was fine, but there at the Hillcrest each communication seemed to deplete my energies and, by 10 o'clock, I could go no further. So I asked if anyone would like to ask me a question. Lots of ladies threw their hands up and one by one I set about answering them as best I could.

The time of 10-30pm announced the end of the demonstration and I was totally done in, I can tell you. I had a sneaky feeling that it was my diet; after all, food creates energy and it takes lots and lots of energy to communicate. But I thought to myself, I'll suffer the loss of energy – maybe it will settle down. But it just didn't. The following night I was in Lytham St. Annes and it was a repeat of what had gone on at Widnes – low energy levels. Yes, communication was absolutely great but I felt feeble at the end. It had been a difficult two nights and slowly, the goal I'd set my sights on, to become super-slim, super-quick, was becoming a pipe-dream. Maybe I'd have to stick at being the oversized me after all.

The following night I had a sitting booked under the name of Angela, who had been recommended to come and see me by the husband of one of my long established hairdressing customers, Joan.

Joan's husband is a photographer and he was filming the wedding of Angela's ex-husband's sister. After seeing her DVD, Angela went to see the photographer to ask if he could produce a DVD of Colin for her. It was he who, after hearing her story about Colin, suggested that she contact Joan's hairdresser whom he described as a very good medium. Subsequently, I spoke to Angela on the telephone and agreed a mutually convenient date and time.

That day I'd tried to eat a little more but not the gross amount I usually consume. A knock prompted me to open the door and a small, light brown-haired lady entered. She seemed timid, quiet and shy.

'Hello, how are you? Come in Angela.' I showed her into my dining room for the sitting. The conservatory was temporarily out of use because we'd had a problem with the roof. Angela looked painfully shy and quiet; and very nervous. As usual, I did all I could to make her sitting as comfortable as possible. I began to open to the Afterworld. I could sense a young man. He was in his late teens, around 17. He had short, clipped hair and seemed very quiet and shy. Already, my energies were beginning to wane again. I didn't know why. It must be that diet, I thought to myself.

Colin, who crossed due to an electrical fault of his heart.

The young man came a little closer to my side. "My name is Colin." 'O.K.,' I said in my head voice. 'Angela, I've a young man here. He is around 17 years of age and he says his name is Colin. Oh, he tells me he is your son.'

'That's true,' she replied. She didn't know what to do, I could see it. Angela didn't know whether to laugh or cry. The sadness that she had lived with was deep; she really did not know how to be happy anymore. As Colin came forward, lots of other people who knew her started to shout to her, giving their name, how they crossed and their relationship to her.

'I am finding it hard to speak to Colin, Angela. He is so quiet and all the others around him are so strong and confident. I just feel my link is weak with him.'

Angela retorted, 'Tell them all to go away, I want to speak to Colin.' However, I couldn't help wondering to myself, if it was caused by me and my low energy problem. As she uttered those words, the people around Colin stepped back and I found myself connecting with him in a far more reliable and acceptable way.

'Colin is showing me that he passed with a condition around his chest area. He is holding his chest too. He tells me he had problems with his heart. He tells me he had an electrical fault in his heart. He says his passing was quick and he passed from this life to the next peacefully. He says he didn't suffer any pain or discomfort.'

'I am amazed, David,' Angela said. 'Colin did have an electrical fault in his heart. Oh my ...' She couldn't finish her words. Angela just stared and smiled.

'Angela, you do understand, don't you, that I could not have known all this beforehand?'

'Yes indeed, I am absolutely stunned.'

For the first time in my sitting, and I wouldn't be surprised if it wasn't the first time since Colin crossed over, Angela smiled a true smile.

'Now he gives me links to Warrington, so there must be a strong connection there. Oh, O.K., he tells me that's where you live.'

'Yes,' Angela whispered.

'But he takes me to Rainford, near St Helens, for strong links too. He is telling me he used to live at Rainford and he went to school there. He is showing me Brooklodge Primary School. Do you understand?' I asked.

'Yes that's right, David.'

'His teacher was Mrs Davenport. Now he is urging me to say, "Do you remember Mrs Davenport, mum?"' I repeated his words. Angela answered, 'Yes, son, I do, she was your teacher.'

'He has said they were great times.'

Angela smiled.

'Colin says he likes your haircut. You've recently had it cut short, haven't you?'

'Yes, I have,' Angela replied. 'Tell him thanks,' she added.

'Oh, now he's telling me you have a hairdresser connection, strongly. Either you're a hairdresser or someone close is, well both really.'

Angela replied, 'I was and so was Colin's dad.'

'O.K. He says you're no longer together with his dad.'

'Correct, David,' she replied.

'You have a new life in Warrington now. Colin gives me the name of Gemma as being close – a sister or girlfriend.'

'Sister, it's his sister's name,' Angela said.

'He sends his love there. He says he misses her very much.'

'Yes, they were very close.'

'Now he links with Ormskirk, Angela.'

'Yes, that's where Colin was born.'

'O.K.,' I replied. Now I could feel my energies beginning to be depleted and I just knew it was time to stop. Colin was stepping back and I didn't want to weaken my communication.

'Angela, I have to stop now, but do you feel good about Colin's communication?'

Angela's answer surprised me totally. 'I do, but I am still not totally convinced, David. I don't mean to be rude and it's not that I don't believe you, it's just I need more.'

'You know, I understand how you feel. If I was in your shoes, I would be the same. I would always need more. I believe it's built in us.'

'Can I come again?' she asked.

'Of course,' I replied.

'Thanks, David.' Angela left and I made my way into the kitchen and tucked into a great big piece of Andrea's home-made chocolate sponge.

'Sod it,' I thought to myself. As long as I can still talk, who cares what I look like?

One night, just a short while after I had done the sitting for Angela, I was sat watching TV, one of those rare occasions I get these days. Suddenly, I was made aware of a young gentleman in the corner of the room opposite me.

'Hello,' I said out loud.

'Hi, I'm Colin.'

'O.K. How are you?' I asked.

'Well, mum's going to call you. Will you fit her in for a sitting,' he asked politely.

'Yes, no problem.'

'Great. Thanks, David,' Colin replied and left.

After the TV programme ended, for no apparent reason, I picked up my mobile phone. There was a new voice message asking for a cancellation or a booking as soon as possible – it was Angela. What was even stranger was that my phone had gone straight to answering machine. It was as if Colin knew I didn't get time to watch TV and he was trying not to disturb me for long.

A few days later, Angela was allotted a cancellation. When she arrived, it was a totally different woman who sat in front of me. She smiled openly. It was nice to see. I could tell the communication had made a difference to her. She sat down, again in the dining room.

'Angela, have you been all right since we spoke last,' I asked.

'Yes, great thanks,' she replied. I could see Colin now moving towards me.

'Hi David,' he said.

'Hello Colin,' I said in my head voice. 'Angela, Colin is here with us. I must ask him to give me a personal detail before he can proceed. Please don't think this is unusual. It is not enough that I can see your son – I must be linked with him properly. I must know, in my heart of hearts, that when you leave this sitting, you do so convinced that I have communicated.

Colin tells me you were painting your kitchen walls the other day. He says the walls were yellow in the kitchen – the colour yellow. Do you understand, Angela?'

I didn't need her to answer really, I could tell by the look on her face. But, as I've said before, the verbal communications help me and the sitter in a positive way.

'He says he is always with you. He was watching you freshening up the walls. He said if he'd been in the physical, he'd have done that job for you.'

She didn't seem to take in what I'd said as she retorted, 'No-one knew what I'd done, no-one. No-one was in the house, no-one knew, even after I'd painted it, because it was overpainted in the same colour and no-one noticed.' At that point, I knew the penny had dropped with her. I continued, 'Colin tells me he has been driving to work with Gemma each morning. He is showing me Gemini Retail Park in Warrington.'

Angela again became silent. She looked down at her paper on my table where she had been taking notes. 'That's where Gemma works, at Gemini Retail Park, Warrington,' she whispered.

'So that tells you that he is watching and he is still around you, doesn't it, love?'

Angela just uttered, 'I'm shocked David.'

'Colin has just said he likes Gemma's car. He really does.'

Angela was again stunned. She simply didn't answer.

'Colin tells me you walk the dogs at the back of your house. He makes me feel there's parkland or waste land at the rear.'

'Yes, that's true, David. It's a park at the back of the house.'

'He tells me that's where you think of him most of all. That is where you go over, in your head, everything that's happened.'

Angela became emotional. 'It's true. I always do that, always. I talk to him there, everything that has happened; I think about it there, it's true.'

'Colin now says, "Don't worry about the dog mum, I've got her here with me, she is fine, much better now. I'm looking after her for you mum."'

'Oh, David. We recently lost our golden retriever dog, Holly. I am so glad he's got her for me. Tell him thanks, David.'

'I don't have to Angela, he can hear you.'

'Thanks, Colin,' she said.

Colin said to me, 'My mum will never get over losing me.' I told her what he'd said and she agreed. I retorted, 'But, by this communication, you will be able to come to terms with your loss and maybe learn to live with it. It is amazing how much a little message helps you to come to terms with the physical loss of a loved one. I use the analogy that if we think of them as emigrated, moved away, but still in contact by phone. O.K., by spiritual phone but still in contact. When you sit in front of a Medium the messages and evidence should be strong for you. If they're not, it simply means that the Medium has not been able to form a strong enough link with your son.'

She thanked me for the advice. 'Now Angela, do you feel I have communicated with Colin in a strong enough way to put you at ease with his crossing?'

She smiled, 'Yes. I'll never get over losing my son, ever, but I feel much better after speaking to him again. Thank you, David.'

Angela left happy with the evidence she had received. I always feel better once I know the person who I am sitting for has felt my help has been of benefit.

Chapter 12

Sussie and Tim

It had been a strange day, a stressful day really. I'd not had a good night's rest because I had been disturbed again. I'd been joined in my sleep by more Spirit Children: Emily, Lucy and Tom and, while I love children, at three in the morning it's not what you need. So I asked Jason to intervene gently and move them on. This he did, bless him. Quietly, he edged them away until they were no longer detectable. Next, I'd been joined at around 4-30am by a face familiar to me, Sussie, my Egyptian guide.

'Hi Sussie, nice to see you.' Sussie was clearly audient to me.

'Hello, David. I'm sorry to disturb you, however, I bring love to you from the Spirit World. Your physical Mediumship has brought peace to so many already but now, your Mediumship will be needed in another direction.'

'O.K., Sussie, how?'

'We will help you to give advice to others. I will work with you.'

'But Sussie, you said we.'

'Oh yes, the other members of my family also will work with you.'

'That's fine Sussie, but with the greatest respect you're only a boy, how can you have the rich experience of life to advise people?'

'No, I am thousands of years old. I have much experience. I have had many reincarnations to Earth, I have lived through many different situations. Trust me when I say I will be able to give you strong advice where your own advice fails.'

'All right Sussie, I'll give it a go,' I said in my head voice not wanting to disturb Andrea.

'So am I to stop communicating with the Spirit People for their loved ones to Earth?'

'No, this guidance, this advice is as well as your Mediumship.'

'Oh boy, more work!' I joked.

'Your rewards will be great,' replied Sussie.

'Thanks, Sussie.'

'Remember, I'll give you confirmation of this conversation in the near future.'

'Very well. I'll look forward to it.'

'Now I'll leave you in peace.'

'Thank you,' I replied. Sussie left. I could feel my face screaming out for sleep. I'd been awake nearly all night. The last thing I remember was 5-30am – as our front door closed when Barry left for the newsagents.

Next Andrea was shaking me. 'Wake up, David, you're going to be late. It's 8-30. We've overslept.'

'Oh, my God.' I jumped up. I looked terrible – pale, white flesh with dark circles around my eyes. To coin a phrase, there was more life in the Afterlife than there was in me. Some might have said, 'Well you have your own business, why don't you phone in and tell them you can't make it in today.' No, it's impossible. I only take sick leave, if I am really very ill. Hairdressing is like a doctor's surgery. People have gone to the trouble of making an appointment for a particular doctor. It is expected that that appointment is to be honoured by that doctor. Illness is excusable, but not sleep deprivation due to chatting with Spirit Children.

So up I got, arriving at 9-20am in my Knowsley Road salon. Josie was reading a magazine as usual. Ann, my 9-30 appointment, walked in at the side of me. Sue came out from the staff room smiling as usual. 'Coffee, David?'

'Please, Sue,' I replied in a tired voice.

'That doesn't sound good, David. I'm glad you're not cutting my hair this morning,' Josie joked.

'Me too, I'd probably chop a finger off,' I replied.

'Tired, love?' Josie asked.

'Yes, shattered, Josie.'

'You're doing too much, far too much,' Josie warned. Josie is a typical mum. She's loving and concerned for everyone. I find that with all my customers, well, I should say friends; I've done their hair for many years, so they are friends. They all understand me completely.

It had been another busy hard morning and the stress came in the afternoon. I must have been overtired. I had taken my mum out for lunch and we had argued all through it. In the end I decided to go home and sleep. The meal had been awful too, both of us ending up feeling slightly unwell after it. I decided to write off the afternoon completely; it had been a disaster and I was to blame. There would have to be an apology to my mother the next day too. That night, to add to it, I was demonstrating in Oldham. Uppermill to be precise, a few miles east of Oldham in an area called Saddleworth. It's amazing what two hours sleep can do for you. I awoke in a different mood altogether, completely different; bright, breezy, oh yes – fantastic.

Eight o'clock soon came around and I stood up and began to communicate. It was only a small audience of around 50 people, but that was no problem either; I like small audiences as well as large. I once arrived at a venue near Runcorn to an audience of 14 – their evidence was overwhelming – and even in recent times at a small venue, only ten turned up on the day after a Bank Holiday. So I worked through and connected for each and everyone in turn, each accepting their loved ones and confirming what they had to say to be correct. O.K., it doesn't usually happen that I only have a small audience but, if it does, it's "carry on regardless".

Anyway, back to Uppermill. The event had gone great guns – 12 messages, all accepted to be correct. Just as my night was coming to an end I was directed to a young man in his early 30s with thick, dark hair, only small, but well-built. He sat alone, quietly watching what was going on.

'Can I come to you, sir?' The man's look changed, his face registering shock.

'I have two gentlemen joining me now, sir. One tells me he is your grandad and one your uncle. Both were very close to you, sir, as you've grown up. They are telling me you are desperate, your life is in turmoil. In fact, out of all these people here, I believe you are the most in need.'

The young man didn't answer with words at first, but broke down into an uncontrollable sob. Looking at him before, he seemed just an ordinary happy-go-lucky young man, yet, in a few seconds, he was an emotional mess.

'Your uncle tells me he used to take you to see Oldham Athletic football matches and he tells me you were such a lovely, young boy. He loved you so much.'

'Yes,' he cried. 'God, help me.' The young man was so emotional that a lady, from the opposite side of the room, came and placed her arms around him, giving him support. Later, I found out she was a total stranger. My heart-felt 'thanks to you my friend', whoever you were; you and your compassion were just what Tim needed at the time.

Next, Tim's grandad gave his name, followed by Tim's uncle. With both names given, Tim became even more upset. His grandad told me Tim was going through a very emotional time involving a separation from his partner and a complete nervous breakdown – Tim was desperate. All this Tim confirmed through his tears, with his new-found friend holding on to him, comforting him.

Tim was at an all time low, suffering from depression and low self-esteem. He'd come along to see if anyone could help him. His pain and torture were immense – he told me he had contemplated ending it all. I could have gone on forever passing personal details from Tim's family in the Afterlife and reeling the evidence off to him and watching his reactions. I've seen some Mediums do that. Whilst it is a form of evidence, to watch someone in need sob so much and for the audience be so taken by the link that they become emotional too isn't really my aim. Tim needed help quickly if he were to survive what life had thrown at him. A Medium revealing his personal problems publicly, in his highly-charged emotional state, wasn't the way to go. So I axed the link.

'I know you are desperate, sir, I promise you this ...' Just as I was about to say the words, 'I'll help you in any way that I can,' Sussie, the Egyptian boy, stepped forward and I couldn't believe the promise I made to Tim. The promise went like this:

'I promise you I'll help you. At the end of this demonstration, stay behind. I will take your name and contact details, then you will come and see me. After one hour of your time, you will feel different. After one month, you will be totally different. You will be a new man.'

'O.K., thank you, sir,' Tim said over and over through his tears. 'Thank you, sir. I've been everywhere. No one has been able to help me, no one. Thank you.'

The audience cheered with elation – many dabbing away their tears of sympathy. I stood there thinking to myself, 'Whatever next?'

A very nervous Tim stayed behind and again I communicated with his loved ones in the Afterworld. Their level of concern was very strong, so I knew we had to move fast. The other problem I had to deal with was Tim's humble ways – if he thanked me ten times, he thanked me ten more, each time calling me 'sir'. 'Thank you, sir.'

Finally, I was on my way home. My day had been long and arduous. I still had to apologise to my mum for all the horrible things I had said over lunch and my distinct lack of care and patience with her. Not to worry, that will be put right tomorrow. Sometimes I'll watch the American Medium, John Edwards. He has a great ability. Again, he is a very different Medium, but still has a strong ability to communicate with the Spirit World. He always ends his shows by telling the viewers to communicate, appreciate and validate your loved ones whilst they're here on Earth, then you don't need a Medium later on to do it for you. I believe these words to be absolutely true and, as my mother's nearly 80, I won't be falling out with her too often at all.

Some days later, Tim came over to my house and sat in the conservatory. We had communicated a couple of times beforehand. Tim, who was nervous about the sitting, wanted to bring his dad, but for some reason unknown to me I was directed to ask him to leave his father outside, in the car on the drive, and to sit alone with me. Again, quite out of character for me, but I was being guided and what I said, *must* happen, if I was to have any success in helping Tim.

Now, what follows is what actually happened. Small details of evidence have been left out, not because Tim chose to leave them out, but because I felt some details are too private for the public forum.

A trembling Tim sat down. 'Why are you shaking?' I asked.

'I don't know. I'm scared of what you're going to do, or say. I've been like this all day, David. Can I call you David, sir?' he asked politely.

'Of course. Is it alright for me to continue calling you Tim?'

'Yes, David.'

'Then we are agreed,' I confirmed. 'Now, I am going to ask out to the Afterworld for any of your loved ones to come forward and any of my guides to come forward who can help you with your situation. Alright?'

'Yes David. Can I just thank you David for all this, what you're doing for me.'

'Once, just once and you've done that already. As all Mediums, we are here to help. No more of that please. I accept your gratitude. Alright?'

'O.K., David,' Tim calmed a little. I could see Sussie stepping forward next to Jason who stood at the side of me.

'Hi Sussie,' I said openly. 'Tim, Sussie is one of my guides and he is here to help you. I am joined also by Jason, my main guide and protector. He will be here on hand, to make sure all we do is completely safe and for your greater good.'

'O.K., David.' Tim again began to relax a little more. You know, watching Tim in my conservatory was just so uplifting. Each time I spoke Tim seemed to relax more and more, until he relaxed so much I could speak to him on a one-to-one level. He calmed down before my eyes.

'Now Tim, my guide tells me you have been finding it very hard to come to terms with the break up of your relationship. He tells me it's been very emotionally taxing for you. He tells me there are issues within this break-up that have hurt you, do you understand?'

'Yes David. Would you like me to say what they are?'

'No, I'll tell you, Tim, if that's all right with you.' Those issues, though common in a lot of break-ups, I must respectfully leave out from my narrative. But, after their confirmation by Tim, my guide wished Tim to go through an exercise with him to help him remove the strong feelings of hurt that he had been living with since the split. Sussie asked Tim to close his eyes and relax. He was to take his mind back to the moment when he had felt hurt the most. Tim followed the instructions and in a moment he was there.

'I'm there, I know I am.'

Then, the guide asked him to relive the moment, speaking his way through it openly as he visualised it and, through his tears, Tim did just that, detail by detail. His pain was evident as his emotions surfaced at every detail – anger, frustration, compassion; it was so awful to watch someone go through this exercise. My heart goes out to others who have to experience such a painful, cleansing process. Tim's anger stopped and peaked at a certain point. Sussie asked him to stop.

'Now Tim, take a piece of paper and write down that particular moment, together with the names involved.'

Tim did this immediately. Sussie then asked him to close his eyes and to relive the whole scenario again up to this point and, once more, describe it out loud in detail. Tim again became very emotional as he relived the moment.

'Stop,' Sussie said loudly. 'What I want you to do next, Tim, is to focus on that paper please and, in a moment, I wish you to give all that anger over to your words on the sheet of paper. All the heartache you have felt, please imagine it has gone from you and it is external to you – it is all on that paper. Inside of you is clear, all of the situation lies on that white paper together with all the pain and suffering that goes with it. Now Tim, you have to make a decision. That decision is whether to keep the paper and its contents for ever, or destroy the paper, thus destroying all that has gone on, for ever. Which will it be, please?'

Tim said, 'I'd like to destroy the paper. I want to move on with my life.'

'Now if you destroy the paper, remember, you destroy the situation and all the emotions that went with it: the pain, torment, the anger, frustration – all will disappear for ever. You still wish this paper to be destroyed?' Sussie asked.

'Yes, totally.'

'Then after a count of three, destroy the paper as best you can. Then, at that point, there must be a new beginning for you.'

After Sussie counted down, Tim vented his anger tearing up the paper into small shreds.

'Now throw it to the floor, Tim,' Sussie said.

'Is that O.K., David?'

'That's what the guide says, Tim, so that's what it's got to be.'

Tim threw it at the floor, his situation scattered into untidy confetti. I looked at Tim.

'How do you feel, Tim,' I asked.

'Don't know quite what to say, David. The word, I think, is 'relieved'. I feel relieved of my burden.'

And I've got to say, he did actually look relieved – the pain of the last couple of years was finally beginning to lift from him.

Next, Sussie asked Tim to look at his situation differently. He explained to him that he was a good person and he would meet someone and settle back down later in his life. He told Tim there would be changes around his job. Again, this came true – just months later.

For some reason Sussie's words gave Tim hope, but also self-belief and self-worth. Tim suddenly exclaimed, 'I feel different already.'

'Do you?' I said, surprised at the sudden exclamation.

'Yes, I do. All my bitterness towards my ex is lifting. Also, I'm looking forward to life, David.' Sussie interjected, 'Ah, but there is one more exercise left, Tim. This exercise you will do daily for the rest of your Earth life, young man.'

Tim looked bemused at there being yet more exercises and, to be honest, with another sitting to go that night, I didn't cherish a repeat of the strong emotions. Isn't it strange? I really don't like seeing young men cry. It hurts me. I can cope with girls crying, but not men. Maybe it's because I am the same sex or something – I can't quite put my finger on it.

Tim was asked to obtain two diaries and label them – one "positive diary", the other "negative diary". At the end of each day, maybe at supper before bed, Sussie asked him to go to that day and in the positive diary list all the positive situations that he had been part of that day, anything at all. For example; I painted a door, it turned out excellently; I talked to an old lady, she felt good afterwards and so did I. Write down anything at all, from waking up to going to sleep. Then, after the positive diary, enter all the negative situations you have felt that day. Such as; the neighbour walked past me without saying 'Hello', she didn't stop I'm boring to talk to; or, I painted a door this morning, but I just can't paint, I'm useless, Sussie continued.

Close your diaries and sleep. At breakfast next day, as you sit at the table, look at your positive declarations and if you feel after reading them they are correct and a truthful representation of the day before, tick them. If they are not, then cross them out. Do the same with the negative diary. You will find if you are honest your mind has tricked you the day before; it has lied to you and, on reflection, the negatives aren't half as bad as you first thought. Again, we must repeat this exercise daily.

Unfortunately Tim, you are like many other young people of your Earth plane: your mind, body and spirit have forgotten how to recognise the positive and negative feelings that we work with and through, each moment of our physical lives. This dissociation with positives and negatives can lead to one totally outweighing the other – usually the negative on top – so then, every situation that we would have faced before, with the balance of both charges, we face with just one, usually negative. By keeping your diary your mind, body and spirit will learn to distinguish those positives and negatives and soon your balance will return once again. You will have harmony but, most of all, peace in your heart and mind. Then Tim again was talked through the example of the exercise. Sussie seemed to leave no stone unturned. He thanked Tim. Tim looked amazing. He was glowing with joy. Next, Tim had some more communication from his loved ones and finally his sitting came to an end. Undeniably, just one hour of my time and his time and the guide's time changed Tim's life, hopefully for ever. Tim has visited me at numerous events. He texts me often with his progress and, trust me, he is a different man altogether. He wants to settle down again, which is understandable – so if anyone out there wants to meet a lovely, kind-hearted young man who is good-looking and is as genuine as the day is long, call me – I know just the guy!

For all of you who have similar problems to Tim, these exercises are easy. Try them, don't let your situation in life beat you, know there is an answer, a way forward. It just takes that moment to make a firm decision to go forward to the door marked "future" and pass through it and, most importantly, close and lock the door behind you.

This chapter is just another example of how my bridge can link adults and their children together. In this particular case, my young guide Sussie helped Tim move on with his life – wonderful.

Letter from Tim Partington

Dear David,
First of all, a big thank you for everything that you and your guide have done over the past months with me. The difference is unbelievable and it just shows how the amazing transformation through you has changed my life for the better.
I was in a clinical mess until I made the trip to Uppermill, then from that night I knew my life was in your hands to get me away from the past and get my new life in order.
The Diary is still going, my outlook on my ex has changed and I know it's only a matter of time when what you have told me will come true.
I go to Uppermill Spiritualist Church every week and my guide, with whom I have connected, is making me a stronger person. The

spirits have even told me about a danger or two that I could face if I don't act on it.

I have met my partner but still waiting for connection. Still without a job, but life will happen thanks to you and I owe you a lot.

If you want to put this in your book, apart from my address, then fine. I hope we will be friends for ever and I think I would love to help you in anything that I can.

I hope your wife is keeping you happy and supporting you forever because I've read most of your book and I wish I will find someone who is strong like her, to help me get to where I should be in life.

Thanks buddy

Tim Partington

Chapter 13

Colin and Angela

After Tim's goodbyes, my next sitting rang the door bell. A lovely-looking, young blonde girl stood at my door. 'Hi, you must be my next sitting.'

'Yes,' she replied coyly.

'Louise?' I asked.

'Yes,' she replied.

'O.K. Louise, if you would like to follow me through into my conservatory.'

Louise didn't say much; she was too busy listening to me – I didn't shut up until I left her in the conservatory to fetch some water for us. She seemed shy and nervous. I was buzzing. Tim's revolutionary change had made me feel good about the spiritual me. The positivity that Sussie had injected into Tim's sitting had rubbed off on me too, I think. I definitely had some spring in my step, that's for sure.

On my way back into the conservatory, I popped my head around the door of the living room. Andrea and Barry sat with dinner on their laps, looking tired. Andrea looked up at me. She'd witnessed what Tim was like before at Uppermill and, on the way out, he'd said 'bye to her. 'Gosh, there was a big difference in Tim, David,' she commented. 'What have you done with him, he was completely different?'

'Thanks, I've got *friends in high places* you see,' I joked. 'See you later.'

'O.K. love,' Andrea replied. Andrea's opinion added a certain strength to my already overwhelming satisfaction borne of Tim's sitting. Louise must have thought I was walking on air or I had a lot of wind, I was smiling so much.

'Hi Louise, it's so nice of you to come along this evening. Have you been to anything like this before?'

She didn't answer, she just smiled, saying nothing.

'But you are in good company with my guides and inspirers who work with me in the Afterworld. Indeed, your loved ones will hopefully come along here today as you have. O.K. Louise, are you ready?'

'Yes, that's fine thanks,' she replied politely.

'Now Louise, I have a young gentleman starting to come close to me. I can't quite see him yet, but he makes me feel very brotherly to you, so this gentleman is your brother. I still can't quite see him enough yet. Sometimes this happens. O.K., he looks around 18 years old. Do you understand?' I asked.

'Yes, my brother was almost 18 years old when he died.'

'Louise, we don't say that word. He's crossed over, made his transition,' I laughed.

'Oh sorry,' she said.

'When he crossed over he was 18 years old, so what I am saying would make sense?'

'Yes, David.'

I always feel I need to verify that what I am saying is true, simply because I can be wrong. I can be totally confused and if I get confused, then my sitter is going to be very confused.

'O.K. Louise, your brother must have been really quiet on Earth; he strikes me, as he draws closer, as being ever so quiet.'

'Yes he was, really quiet,' she confirmed.

'O.K. now, I'm still not seeing him clearly, which is unusual I have to say, but maybe I'm having a blind day,' I joked.

'He tells me he had an electrical fault in his heart, he tells me his heart gave up in the end, do you understand?'

'Yes, I do,' She replied.

'He gives me the name of David, he keeps saying the name David and so your brother's name is David.' But before she could comment it was almost as if the young man lifted a net curtain from my eyes and I could see him clearly.

'Hold it Louise, don't say a word, I've seen you before young man.'

The lad smiled and said, 'Yes mate, I'm Colin, my name is Colin.'

'Louise, your brother is Colin and he's been working with me before, he tells me.'

'That is his name,' a stunned Louise replied.

'Colin is giving me a birthday card to give to someone very close right now.'

'Oh yes, that will be for my mum, it's her birthday in the next few days.'

'Yes, he puts his thumb up. Send her his love, please Louise.'

'O.K., I will tell her,' she replied.

'He keeps giving me the name of David. I don't know whether he is addressing me or it is for someone else.'

'I know why, David,' she replied.

'Colin tells me you have brought his watch with you, it's in your bag.'

'Yes it's here. Should I show you?'

'No,' I replied. 'The confirmation that you have it with you now in your bag is fine by me, that is all I need to know. Oh, now Colin is describing the watch to me – it's really chunky, it has silver buttons all the way around the face. It's quite a heavy-looking watch. Colin says he loved that watch.'

'Yes, the description is correct,' said Louise.

'O.K.,' I said. '*Now* you can show me the watch.'

She removed the watch from her bag and sure enough it was the same as I had described it. Colin looked at me and said, 'That's my favourite watch, David.' I repeated his words to Louise. All the way through the sitting, Colin kept repeating the name Gemma until the penny dropped with me that Louise's other name was Gemma. I didn't mention to her that I knew that she had given me another name because some people prefer to book under false names – it just removes the directness of the communication away from themselves. So I thought no, leave the name as Louise, so I did. I told her that Colin wasn't so happy with what he described as her current relationship and I said to her neither was she. Louise confirmed this as being correct. I then told her this was where the connection to David fitted in.

'Yes,' she replied.

'Colin says he loves your flat, Louise. It's got laminate floors all through and a lovely beige settee. He says he's been having a look around.'

'Yes, that describes my place, David. Has he been looking around whilst I've been in or when I've been at work?' she asked.

Colin replied both, but mostly when she had been at work. She seemed bothered about this.

'Does he watch all the time?'

'To be honest, it's a question most people need to know an answer to when they discover their loved ones watch them. Just to put you at ease, unless you were some sort of strange person, you wouldn't really want to watch someone sitting on the toilet in the physical, so why would you want to watch them when you were in the non-physical. In the Spirit World, you are usually with a loved one or even a few loved ones, so you wouldn't want to watch, or be seen watching, your relative having a shower, for instance, or in their more intimate moments – if you get my drift.'

Louise laughed out loud. 'Well, that's okay then,' she said jokingly. We both burst out laughing again.

'Just to change the subject, Louise, Colin has just informed me that someone is reading my first book *Friends in High Places*.'

'Yes, it's my mum,' she replied.

'Great, I hope she enjoys it.'

'Sadly Louise, we must bring this sitting to an end. Colin says he hopes it works out in your relationship. He'll be looking out for you. Oh, and good luck in your new job.'

She looked confused, but I could only say what Colin had said to me. 'It's been a real eye-opener, David,' she said. 'I'd never have believed that you could have contacted my brother in this way. It's marvellous, thanks a lot.'

'It's no problem Louise, or is it Gemma?' She looked shocked. I knew the real reason why she had booked under a different name, but that's fine by me. Plus, it wasn't only confirmation for Gemma and Angela, it was also confirmation for me as well. Gemma looked at me and smiled. 'It's my other name; some people call me Gemma and some people call me Louise.'

'Oh I see,' I replied. 'Well, thanks anyway. Can I call you Gemma then please?'

'Yes, that's fine David,' she replied.

'O.K., we'll hope to see you again sometime Gemma. Oh, Colin's shouting, "'bye Gemma. 'Bye, tell mum I love her, love you too, bye-bye Gemma."'

'Bye Colin,' she said quietly. As I showed Gemma to the front door she thanked me again. 'It's been really great, thanks David,' and she left.

Closing the front door, I made my way into the lounge. Barry had gone to bed and Andrea lay asleep on the couch. 'Andrea, you okay love?'

'Yes,' she whispered. 'I'm just tired. Barry went to bed after Tim left. He's got to be in work at 5am. There's some dinner in the microwave if you're hungry.'

'O.K. love, thanks,' I said, kissing her forehead. As I stood in front of the microwave, watching my supper go around as it heated up, Colin came forward and thanked me for everything. He said he couldn't have been happy and settled until he knew his mum and sister were. He said his mum was great, she was moving on a little and he couldn't thank me enough. I turned and said to him that I'd enjoyed it too and he was a great communicator and I looked forward to communicating for him again in the future. Colin thanked me again politely and left.

I smiled. You know, some people to the Earth think what I do is a sin, a really bad sin. I still don't understand that school of thought or that sentiment – whether it came from the Good Book or any other source. I communicated strongly, giving absolute evidence of Colin's survival, Angela and Gemma were now able to move on a little, they felt happier after what I'd done.

Some time had passed since Gemma approached me for the first time and, as I said before, I'd been struggling to make contact with the particular people I wanted to go into my book. Angela's son, Colin, was one such sitting. More than a year had gone by and, trust me, it takes so long to get everyone together. All of a sudden I received a text from Gemma asking to speak to me. Obviously, I was elated as you can imagine. I arranged to meet Gemma so I could ask her to ask her mum, Angela, to get in touch with me. Gemma obliged. At that meeting, Colin graced us with his presence again; he was so strong now, he only needed a physical body and he would have been alive in the fullest sense.

'Gemma, Colin's here, he says 'Hi'. He is overjoyed that he is going in my book – he feels good about it.'

'Tell him my mum will be overjoyed with the news. I can't wait to get home and tell her,' she replied.

'Gemma, have you had some recent dental work or is someone around you having a problem with their teeth?'

'No,' she replied. 'I can't think of that. No, sorry, not as I know of.'

'Well, he is drawing my attention to your teeth and I know there will be a reason for this. Hold on Gemma, I'll ask him to make it clearer to me because the comment is about teeth, I know it is.'

'Colin, what do you mean?' I asked. Colin replied, 'Tell Gemma I love her teeth; eventually, mine would have been like that.' Later, she realised Colin had braces on his teeth when he passed to the Spirit World.

'Now he tells me, Gemma, you have a new car; he really loves it. He thinks it's great. He says your mum was looking at cars in a garage in Warrington the other Sunday.'

'That's right,' Gemma replied. 'I do have a new car and yes, my mum was looking at cars in the garage the other Sunday.'

'He tells me one of your mum's ambitions is to run her own dog kennels.'

'She would really love that, it would really make her very happy,' she answered. 'Mum would love that, she loves dogs. They're her escape in life.'

What happened next was another of those priceless moments involving physical Mediumship. Colin decided to cause a perfectly round circle of what appeared to be condensation on my conservatory window. He then tried to put his handprint in the condensation. This was really strange as none of the other windows was steamed up, only the patch that Colin had caused. I asked him to stop as it might scare Gemma. At first he wouldn't and then he did what I asked and stopped. I have no idea how he achieved this effect and I know the scientific mind would not support this happening, but we both witnessed it. During this occurrence I kept Gemma informed. Simply, I didn't want it to scare her or make her feel uncomfortable. Gemma turned around and looked at the windows. She could see what Colin was up to and that all the other conservatory windows were clear, but instead of being hysterical she was calm, smiling at what he was trying to do. The truth is, I think Colin got fed up when he couldn't get the print on the condensation; nevertheless, it was absolutely obvious what he was up to.

Colin then made reference to Gemma being much happier in her new relationship. She confirmed this to be correct. He put a congratulations sign above her head. Colin clarified that the congratulations were to do with her engagement. Again she confirmed this information to be true.

'He tells me, Gemma, that you've changed your job again since we last spoke and you're much happier, although you're always on the look out for something better.'

'Yes, David,' she confirmed. 'I am always on the look out for a different job.'

'Now, Gemma, I'm shown a little miscarriage in the Spirit World. Colin tells me he has a little boy with him. He didn't quite make it to Earth and I want to say his transition back to the Spirit World was in recent months.'

She looked shocked. 'Yes, that's right. A friend of mine had a miscarriage a couple of months ago.'

'Colin tells you to smile, the boy is fine. He's got him and he is looking after him.'

Gemma kept composed. 'Thank you,' she replied.

Whenever I deliver any news about miscarriages I like to get more information, but in some cases you know how far to go with the link. Just intimating to Gemma about the little boy and the fact that Colin was taking care of him was far enough.

Colin just had to be in this book; his ability to communicate at times overwhelmed me. His caring and positive nature with his parent and his sister just added weight to my decision to include him. Love can build a bridge between physical life and the non-physical life.

Angela and Gemma, Colin is a star. He has certainly left a lasting impression on me. Thank you and God bless you always for allowing me to tell the world about your wonderful son and brother.

To all bereaved parents out there, I say, have hope. Always remember, your children are only a moment from you, at any time, when they are in the Afterworld. Sometimes, I've sat watching TV or reading a book and, out of the corner of my eye, I've caught sight of movement and that movement, that vision which my ordinary human eye has captured, is the physical movement in the Afterworld.

These people in my book are real people, who have suffered real pain, as probably the majority of my readers have. I can never bring back your dear loved ones, I can only give you hope in the absolute fact that your loved ones can be contacted in the Afterworld, if you so choose and if they choose to communicate. In this modern world, why should we allow old-fashioned beliefs or prejudices to stop us gaining comfort? Our world is a sad enough place at present with the awful wars and unrest which take place. In addition, there are all the unfortunate people who make their transition from this life to the next, due to malnutrition, Aids or other diseases. Yes, all of you out there, if you can't face going along to a Medium and communicating with your loved ones, I hope that simply reading my book will give you some peace in your hearts and comfort in the knowledge that they live in the Afterworld. They watch you and try, mostly, to take part in your life, in a non-physical sense. Some even try to give you signs, as Colin did. The one main point is this: never, ever give up hope that you will one day hear from, or see, your child again.

Angela Morris – How Meeting David Has Helped Me

I am the type of person who needs very specific evidence before I truly believe in anything. My logical brain kicks in and I find good reasons why people may have come to that conclusion.

After meeting David I feel he has provided me with enough accurate personal evidence that no-one else could know. I now have the proof I needed to help me carry on in this world without Colin in the physical sense. I now know Colin is still with us and this has brought me so much comfort and given me the strength to carry on, which has got to be a good thing.

I feel better knowing Colin is happy with his new life and look forward to the day when I will be re-united with my lovely son. Thank you David, for contacting Colin and you have helped me so much.

I am now very involved with the charity Sudden Arrhythmic Death Syndrome UK* which raises awareness about the condition which robbed me of my lovely son.

I have spoken in public about losing Colin, something I never thought I would ever do, but I now believe Colin is close by and guiding me in this direction. By talking about Colin at these events means his memory lives on and his untimely passing wasn't in vain.

Angela Morris

* For more information about the condition SADS UK go to www.sadsuk.org

Chapter 14

A nasty shock, then Paula

The physical side of Mediumship has never really appealed to me; however, I know from my own experiences that that side of my gift really does exist. In June, 2005, we enjoyed a holiday in France and I discovered the physical side of my Mediumship. That was when the Spirit World informed me and confirmed that I was a physical Medium, as well as a mental Medium. My physical Mediumship has surfaced and showed itself in many different ways since and later I'll tell you about one of my most moving experiences using that aspect of Mediumship.

We've been going along to Briars Hall, Lathom for years, not only demonstrating there but also patronising their restaurant. Sue, Karen and the staff there have always made us feel very welcome. After my visit to Briars Hall, I began to talk to one of the staff members, Sue.

Sue had come along to the demonstration and she had received absolute evidence that life is continued after the physical body dies. Sue requested a private one-to-one sitting; she wanted to have contact with her father and other family members. She wanted her family to sit in on the reading, so we arranged just that.

During the sitting Sue and her family appeared nervous, especially her son-in-law, who struck me as a total sceptic. As the evidence began to flow for Sue and her family, a very heartbreaking story came out and Sue and her family were moved by the detailed reading I passed to them from the Spirit side of life.

In that reading, I gave some absolutely amazing evidence to her son-in-law. It was even mind-blowing for me, yet I was only the deliverer. Just imagine how he received it, a sceptic who had never had any dealing with a Spirit Medium before. His life was all business-related, even his friends were all linked to his business. At the end of the sitting, the Spirit asked that Sue's son-in-law return alone as they wished to do a strictly one-to-one sitting. I couldn't imagine why; I was given no indication by the Spirit World whatsoever. Sue's shell-shocked son-in-law agreed to come back. He was so blown away by the first sitting who knows what the second one had to offer.

The Spirit World was not to disappoint us. The following Friday, Sue's son-in-law arrived alone and again received absolutely brilliant communication. The advice about his business and its growth far exceeded any knowledge that a human being could offer. Again, he was completely speechless. I would have been too – except that I was the one who was mediating for him.

It was what followed that gave me a clue something was changing in my Mediumship. In our conservatory, that place where all my sittings are held, there was, in the centre, a clear-glass-topped coffee table. It was mounted on a wooden frame and had wheels. I've just recently got rid of it. Whilst it was great when we had guests over at Christmas or on other occasions, most people seemed to bang their shins on its edges and that used to go through me (as well as them).

However, before its removal and as Sue's son-in-law received his reading, the coffee table, to my amusement, decided to move position. I stopped in mid-flow and a totally-flummoxed man looked at me and, rather stunned, he just asked, 'That coffee table has just moved, hasn't it?' 'Yes,' I replied. He gave out a very nervous laugh which, if you hadn't been part of the situation, you would have said seemed put on, but it was real. I just looked at him and joked, 'Well you are in the presence of your loved ones on the other side; maybe they want you to know it's really happening.' He smiled and we continued the sitting.

Again at the end, he seemed completely stunned by the whole sitting. Truly, it had converted him, but all this physical evidence was leading up to a very different situation.

Later that month, I was conducting another one-to-one reading in the conservatory. As I was giving the evidence to the young lady who sat in front of me, the room became very foggy. The atmosphere felt so different in the conservatory. It reminded me of sitting in my car on a winter's morning and the windows steaming up around you. The lady, again a sceptic, couldn't understand or rationalise why it was happening. Then the windows became dotted all over, just like wallpaper; an almost continuous pattern – even I thought it to be strange.

In the end, she became so fazed by it she decided to leave and ended the sitting very early. As she left, the windows returned to normal. She had received absolutely perfect evidence of Spirit, but that little unexplained occurrence had really put her off and no matter how I tried to put her at ease, she was uncomfortable and, in the end, decided it wasn't for her.

These happenings recurred on a much more regular basis during the sittings. One lady experienced her Spirit cat rubbing up against her leg as she received a message from her husband in the Afterworld. She was very comforted by this. The cat had only crossed over days before and she was astounded by the description that I gave of her cat, simply because there was one unusual feature that it had – one half of a back leg was missing due to a very bad accident it had been involved in some years before. Together with this information and the physical experience the cat had given, the entire sitting had changed her belief system. It gave the lady hope. It later emerged she was suffering a terminal illness and the fear she'd lived with every day since her diagnosis, had been diminished by her reading. Sadly, some five months later, she herself crossed over. Her family, were strongly against me giving more details, so, respecting their wishes I have restricted myself to this short passage. I thank them for their honesty and for their permission to use what I have.

So it was clear to me the physical side of my gift was developing. The reason would soon become apparent. Thursday evening came round again and I decided to go to the Purple Light Spiritualist Church. I'd never heard of the Medium who was demonstrating that night but I decided I'd go along anyway. Each demonstration teaches you something more. The demonstrator's philosophy was all about physical Mediumship and how she had been influenced in her life by that particular aspect of her gift. She talked about the different physical Mediums she knew personally and described in detail their particular gifts. The talk was very interesting and a lot of what she was saying I could relate to with my own development in the physical aspect of Mediumship.

She then began her demonstration. 'Can I come to you, my dear?' she said pointing over to me.

'Yes. Thank you,' I replied.

'I am seeing the colour purple around you, dear,' she said. Well, what answer could I give, only yes, simply because being a Medium I do understand why she would relate the colour purple with me?

'Now sir,' she continued. 'I can see spirituality, so I am looking at a spiritual gentleman. Do you understand?'

'Well, yes,' I replied. I am in a spiritualist centre so it's a nine-out-of-ten chance that I am likely to be a spiritual person.

'Now I am seeing a tower, a very tall tower. I am seeing you climbing up to the top of the tower. Each set of steps is a different colour – red steps, then a balcony then orange steps, then a balcony, next yellow steps turning to green, then blue and then the blue darkens into purple. Can you understand why I say this to you sir?'

'Yes,' I replied. Sometimes I climb the imaginary tower in my meditation. The colours represent my Chakra points. I answered only 'Yes' I might add.

'The information in the way of my explanation is for your benefit only. Now sir, I see white around you and I feel you are illuminated, so I believe you are a Medium.'

'Yes,' I replied.

'I am told you are experiencing changes in your development. These changes would be with the physical aspect of your Mediumship.'

'Correct,' I replied.

'I am told you will be a physical Medium, sir. I am told you will work in this field only. This is what the Spirit World wishes for you.'

'Oh,' I replied. I didn't know quite what to make of that statement, simply because the choice seemingly had been made for me by the Spirit World. I had no say and that is something I simply will not accept – if I am going to do this work then the Spirit World must accept that I will decide how I work, where I work and when.

You may say, 'That's a little controlling of you, David.' However, I believe you get the choice anyway but, according to my friend on the rostrum, my future development was set in aspic. No fear, I thought to myself. She then continued with my life path and how Spirit had chosen my route of development. Finally, she ended by inviting me to talk to her at the end: she had more to say about the physical Mediumship. She then moved on.

I couldn't wait for the service to end. I wanted to ask the lady about the spirits apparently making life-changing decisions without me being consulted first. I believe the choice should be mine. O.K., I am only ordinary without this gift and, as I've stated on many occasions, I wouldn't be without my gift, but I must insist to the Spirit World that I, always, must be in control.

The service came to an end. It was my belief that the philosophy was far more interesting than the Mediumship, but that is just my opinion on the hour or so that I'd experienced. I walked forward to the lady who pleasantly shook my hand. 'I can tell you are such a strong, physical Medium. It's lovely to feel your energies,' she said closing her eyes as she spoke.

I was tingling through my body from my head to my feet. 'Oh yes, I can tell you're very gifted,' she went on. 'I'd love to meet you sometime to discuss it in depth; there are pitfalls with physical Mediumship you know.'

'Oh, what would they be?' I asked curiously.

'Well, you don't have a long, physical life span because it uses all your energies. Your life span is affected. I rarely know a physical Medium who makes it past 60.'

'Really?' I replied hesitatingly.

'But I am happy to tell you the gift of physical Mediumship is yours.'

I remember those words being said to me with all the conviction of a well-rehearsed play and, stunningly, she'd crowned my so-called gift with a death sentence. All in the line of duty, I think. So I could give my people the physical experience of Spirit but, as a reward for my dedication and trust, I'd cross over myself before I reached the age of 60!

'What an opportunity I am given – it's psychic suicide,' I joked, but she didn't laugh. Very quietly and very seriously she looked at me and said, 'You have been chosen.'

'Thanks,' I replied. 'Thanks for the advice,' I smiled and walked away. Well, I didn't expect that little lot in my reading, I thought. June walked over to me smiling.

'What's up love, you look deep in thought, David.'

'I am. The Medium has just told me I am going to be a physical Medium only, this is what the Spirit World has decided and what's more, to top it off, physical Mediums live very short lives. Usually, they are crossed before they're 60.'

'Sixty?' June looked horrified. 'Rubbish,' she said. 'Absolute rubbish, David.'

'Do you think so, June?' I asked as her words began to sink in even more.

'Yes, I think it's utter rubbish. The Spirit World gives you choices. They only want you to work the way you feel and enjoy working the best. They would support your decision, if you absolutely wish not to work in a certain way and, as to it being harmful and detrimental to your life span, well, I just don't believe it. To be quite honest David, I know many Mediums who are physical or otherwise, some well into their 80s. Now, what you need to do is speak to Jason, your guide, and see what he has to say.'

'Yes I do, June,' I replied. 'After all, I am happy with my physical life and although I know one day I'll have to make my transition, I really don't want to speed it up. I want just to go when it's my turn, naturally.'

'Of course you do, love,' June reassured me. 'And you're going nowhere,' she followed. 'The Spirit World needs you to do a lot more work for them yet here on Earth, David, a lot more.'

'It's twaddle, isn't it?' She smiled one of those smiles. What she was giving me was what I call a "June professional opinion" look – no incriminating words, no opinions, just a reassuring "you're not wrong" smile.

'I'll let you know what Jason says,' I replied.

'Yes, you do that love. Give me a call.'

And with that I left. I decided that if my life span was going to be affected, I'd better not stay for the open circle – I'd better get home and make the most of my family and my possessions. Now, you're all thinking to yourselves that I'm making fun, aren't you? Well no, I am not. Quite seriously, the fact that I thought in this way and have revealed those thoughts, should give you an under-standing of the magnitude of responsibility that is placed upon practising Spirit Mediums. I was troubled, to say the least, and immediately when I got home explained to Andrea and Barry what had been said. They know me best and suggested that I should speak to Jason and ask his advice on this matter.

Without a moment to lose, I made my way into the conservatory and opened up to the Spirit World, using a simple meditation technique. Jason sat waiting for me.

'Hello Jason,' I said.

'Hello David,' he replied. 'I'd like to make you very clear on something.' Jason, my guide, can talk to me in so many different ways, through thoughts and feelings, or by simply shaping my lips and using my voice-box to form words. Because I recognise this as not being my own doing, not even my own sensing, I can rely on the answer to my questions being absolute and therefore the guidance is more reliable. Because the answers to me are so clear, it is almost impossible for my imagination to pollute our communication.

Now, going back to my communication with Jason, without any hesitation I looked at him and said openly, 'Jason, I'm not very happy tonight. I've heard from another Medium at the Purple Light Church that the Spirit World has chosen me to be a physical Medium only – this is how they intend me to work in the future. Then the Medium told me that physical Mediumship would cut down my intended physical life span on the Earth plane. She said physical Mediums only live until they are around 60, if they are lucky. Jason, is this true?' I could feel myself becoming stressed. This is a feeling I am not used to when communicating with the Spirit World.

Before Jason could answer I followed my outburst with, 'If it is, that you have chosen me to work in a way I simply have no interest in, then the Spirit World can think again, because I won't do it, plus I don't want my life cut short. Sorry Jason, I don't.'

Jason just looked at me; then I could feel and sense every word of his reply.

'The Spirit World loves you working for them, they would never force you to work in any other way than that which suited you and, most importantly, you felt comfortable with. Spirit World cannot give and take away life, simply because they are life, they are the true life. If we treated the Medium in such a way, forcing our will upon them and removing their freedom of choice, then I would say that, sadly, we would have very few Mediums left. So my answer is, yes, the physical element of your Mediumship is there to use, if you so choose, but only alongside your communication, as is the healing gift. The use of one's gift correctly will never shorten your life span, but enhance it. These gifts, used in the correct way, can only be for the betterment of your fellow man.'

A sense of relief came over me. 'Thank you Jason,' I replied. Jason smiled and said, 'is there anything else that I can help you with David?'

'No, no thanks Jason. I'm happy with what you have said.' With that I thanked Jason and then using a simple technique I closed down to the Spirit World.

It's always a true saying, 'if in doubt, ask out' – you will always find the truth in your guide's words. It was from those kind words spoken by Jason that I decided I wasn't going to be fazed by whatever the Spirit World would put in my path. You know, one thing is certain, when you set out on your spiritual path there is never a dull moment. You simply don't know what is around the corner.

The time had soon come around for my Liverpool event. The New Year already seemed to be flying by – at this rate it would soon be Christmas again, I thought to myself. Liverpool welcomed me for the first time that season. The room was full to bursting.

It was coming time for me to start the evening. I'd requested all my guides and inspirers to come forward to help me with the communication. After speaking to each one and thanking them for joining me, Jason stepped close to me.

'Hi, Jason,' I said.

'Hello, David,' he replied.

'I feel a little low on energy tonight, Jason. Can you help?' I asked.

'Don't worry, David, we will sort it out for you.'

'Thanks. Will you work strongly with me tonight, Jason? Can I see the Spirit people clearly please?'

'You will see the Spirit people crystal-clearly – clairvoyantly,' Jason replied.

'Can I hear the Spirit people clearly please?' I asked.

'You will hear the Spirit people clairaudiently and, again, very clearly, David.'

'Thank you Jason, and can I sense the Spirit people very clearly, Jason?'

'You will sense the Spirit very clearly – clairsentiently,' he replied.

'Jason, can I move direct to the correct people I need to be with?'

'Of course,' Jason replied confidently. 'You will move directly and each time will be 100% correct. Please trust,' he added.

'O.K., Jason,' I replied feeling a little more calm now. Please remember it takes a lot of confidence to get up on the stage and do what I do. It's not like an actor who can rehearse his lines or a dancer who rehearses steps; every communication is different and, again I must repeat that, as a Medium, you are only as good as the person in the Spirit World is with regards to communication and details.

Jason was really close to me now. To give you some idea of what I mean by "close", think of someone standing next to you – shoulder to shoulder – that is Jason's position. When I am joined by a Spirit person who isn't within my unit, *ie* someone else's loved one, they stand the other side of Jason. As the link becomes stronger Jason will step back a little to let them closer, but they never get as close as Jason is to me, ever.

To return to my pre-demonstration check, which was taking place in the room at the side of the stage, I opened my eyes and an energy rush passed straight through me from the crown of my head to the tips of my toes and fingers. I just tingled and buzzed – it was as if I had drunk 30 cans of Red Bull. Something happened that night in that room that I've never experienced before or since, but if you could have plugged electric lights into me, I am sure I'd have illuminated all of Blackpool, even Vegas – I was like Superman.

But that wasn't the only first-time surprise Spirit had in store for me that night – what followed topped everything. I could not have expected ever to witness, or to have been lucky enough to be part of, that evening.

After the preliminaries of introducing myself and putting people at ease explaining what to expect, I began to work. I moved over to a large, blonde lady who was seated in the centre aisle. She was surrounded by a party of about six or eight people. I began to bring her mother through to her. The communication was very strong and the level of information so strong and detailed it was amazing. She had had such a difficult life, my heart bled for her. She was one of those people you wanted to walk up to and put your arms around and say, 'Come here love, I'll make everything right for you.' Strangely enough and I say that because it doesn't often happen, the lady's mum brought forward a man who directed me to another lady, still in the centre aisle, but she was sitting maybe ten or twelve seats away from the blonde lady. I moved to that lady and started to communicate with her dad in the Spirit. She, too, had been having a rough time with her marriage and, in the end, she'd split up from her husband and her dad was wishing her good luck with her new life in Murcia, southern Spain. She was overjoyed to have received such strong communication. The link had meant she could move on. She'd not been present when her dad had died and she had not been able to come to terms with her absence, after being so close to him.

I thanked the young lady and wished her well with her new life abroad. As I was about to move on, the gentleman directed me to a lady in a black-and-white striped top, still on the same table but at the opposite end. I couldn't believe it; it was as if the spirits were keeping me in one part of the room. So, jokingly, I said to the rest of the audience, 'Sorry guys, you lot have wasted your money tonight; it's all happening here,' and I pointed to the centre. Everyone laughed; it broke the intensity of what had gone before.

The lady in stripes shook as she took hold of the audience microphone. 'Hello, David love,' she said in a very nervous, quivering voice.

'Hello, love. Are you nervous, sweetheart?' I replied.

'Yes love, it's because I don't know what you're going to say to me,' she retorted.

'Only good things, my love,' I replied.

'Thank you, David. God bless you, love.' As she said those words, the man in the Spirit related to the younger lady stepped aside and I was joined by another gentleman. He had crossed with lung cancer and it turned out to be the lovely woman's other half. She was elated. The link was super. He brought through her mother and father, her brother and uncles – a full family joined me from the Afterworld to talk to this one woman and her son. The room was electric; it was so much fun it almost felt as though the Spirit World was lifting the atmosphere with laughter, preparing us for what was to come.

I ended my link with the lady on the centre aisle. The room broke into a rapturous round of applause. Well, the Spirit hadn't failed to deliver on that table. With the depth of communication and the importance of each link, time had gone over – I can usually give five or six messages in my first half, but time had disappeared and we went into the interval.

During the interval I began to communicate again with my guide Jason, running through the previous links and asking if there was anything I could have done to make them better. After our conversation, Jason made me aware that my first link in the second half would be different – a special moment.

'But how?' I asked.

'Trust,' Jason replied.

'Please tell me.'

Jason smiled and repeated the word, "trust". It was obvious to me that I wasn't going to get out of him what was going to happen. It seemed that this was going to be another test of my inner strength and trust.

In the second half of the demonstration, I opened up again by putting the audience at ease. I was directed right to the back of the room to a dark-haired lady in a stripy top with her daughter sitting at the side of her. The lady looked "dropped on" as she was passed the microphone. I began to bring a gentleman through, describing him in detail. The lady confirmed she knew the gentleman and that what I was saying was correct. What was odd about this link was I didn't know who the man was. He gave me barely any evidence, but the small bits he did give were detailed, accurate and confirmed by the lady. My solar plexus was just jumping out of my body and at first I thought this man must have had problems in that direction before he crossed. Your solar plexus is a Chakra point in the centre of your tummy area. It is where you experience "gut feelings".

I was about to find out why my solar plexus was jumping out so much. The gentleman in the Afterworld said to me audiently, 'Tell them I have the boy, please David.'

'O.K., I will,' I replied.

'He wants you to know he has the boy.' Before the words left my lips I could see a little boy aged 4 to 4½ years. He was a beautiful little soul with brown hair. He directed me to her daughter at the side of her who, at this point, sat motionless.

'Love, I need to come to you. This is your child, your little boy. He's shouting mummy and nanny. He's waving.'

'Oh my God,' the girl screamed. The room fell into silence. Every person seemed moved by this link. All you could hear were the sobs of a heartbroken mother. Jason told me the boy wanted to touch his mum and I must trust. Oh goodness, I thought, what's going to happen. Then, as Jason said the words to me, the boy's mother shouted, 'Can you see him, David? Can you see him?'

'Yes,' I replied, then I described him in detail and she was absolutely heartbroken.

Then the girl pleaded, 'Can you touch him, David, can you touch him?'

Before I could think, the words that left my lips were, 'No, but you can.'

'Oh, my God,' she cried.

'Come up to the front,' I beckoned. The girl made her way over to me. Barry put a chair down about seven or eight feet from me. The girl sat down. The room was silent. My solar plexus just expanded into a tube of energy. I coaxed the little boy forward; it was as if the energy from my solar plexus was helping the little one come forward. 'Come on, little fellow,' I said, 'go over to mummy.' I gave the audience a running commentary as the boy walked over and touched his mum's face. The girl screamed with emotion and delight; people wept openly. How I controlled my own emotions, I just don't know!

'He's touching me, I can feel him,' she screamed. 'I can.' I could feel the little boy's energies start to deplete.

'He has to stop now,' I said gently to the lady.

'I love him so much,' the girl was very emotional. As he stepped back, my solar plexus retracted back to normality. The room cheered and clapped through the tears. There wasn't a dry eye in the house. The young lady had to be led out. It was obvious to me the whole link had just become too overwhelming for her to bear. I knew now why the Spirit World had been preparing me. I don't think I would have been able to cope with the magnitude of what had just happened if I hadn't been broken into the idea first. Through me, the Spirit of a young boy had been able to make physical contact with his mother. How humbled I felt to be chosen by the Spirit World to do this for another human being. Undeniably, I was able to bring a child, a little boy, forward and, using my energy, he was able to touch his mother's face. Well, thank you Spirit World, thank you for choosing me as your vessel to do this.

This was the first time, but not the last, that I was given this privilege by the Spirit World. The young girl was Paula and she reacted to this situation as any loving mother would. It was some weeks later that she communicated how she had felt, about the whole experience, by placing a message on my website's 'Guest Book'. What Paula hadn't realised was that little Sam had changed a part of my Mediumship for ever. I can only ever thank Paula and little Sam for allowing me to be the bridge between angels. I just know Paula and Sam's story will give a lot of bereaved parents hope. For every one of us who have loved and lost, little Sam is an inspiration to us all.

Paula's Message

My beautiful, perfect, dark-haired, 6lb. 12oz. baby boy was born on 20 May 2002 at 7-52pm. Sam Ian Kenneth Swinnerton, named after his father and grandfather, was christened the following day; all in white he looked so small and precious. On 29 May 2002, Sam was buried in a tiny white coffin, dressed in his best clothes surrounded by toys, photos, love, but most of all millions of tears. This was my first pregnancy and everything was perfect. All scans showed that my baby was doing everything he should be and so we bought everything, decorated his room, packed all the hospital bags and just sat and waited.

On Sunday 19 May, my husband was at work and I can only describe that I didn't feel 'right', something was wrong. My husband drove me to the maternity ward, the midwives didn't look too concerned; they knew me and how well I was doing.

They scanned my belly – nothing.

I looked at my husband; tears were streaming down his face. The doctor confirmed, 'I'm so sorry, he's not there any more.'

I hate this word – 'stillborn' – but that was my SAM, born the following day, no reasons, no explanations, total shock from all doctors and midwives. But only now do I understand that my son was special, extra special – he was needed as an angel and that's why God picked him.

I went to David Traynor's evening with my mum. I had been once before and enjoyed it so much that I took my mum along to witness what I had previously.

After the interval David said he wanted to speak to the dark lady in the stripy top. This was my mum. Mum held the microphone as David described a gentleman who had passed. Mum recognised this man almost straight away. But then David turned to me, 'It's you I need to speak to, this gentleman's brought a small boy with him, your boy.'

The only way I can describe how I felt was a massive explosion of fear, excitement, amazement and desperation. I so wanted to contact my son.

David told us that this boy was waving to his mummy and nanny. I shouted, 'Can you see him?' 'Of course,' was David's reply and he described my son just as I imagined him to look now.

'Can you touch him?!' I screamed back. 'No', said David, 'but you can.'

David told me to come up to him on the stage and sat me down on a chair about seven feet away from him. I haven't shaken so much, been so desperate.

'He will touch you now, you will feel him,' David said. 'Will you be all right?'

'Yes, yes,' I screamed through the tears, shakes and emotions. David spoke and beckoned my little one to me. 'Go and see your mum, little fella.'

As I sat the whole room around me was so still, silent, people crying, looking amazed, shocked. My son's two little hands pressed my cheeks and I felt my baby, exactly how my two children now touch my face when playing.

The experience only lasted seconds. I was screaming and grabbing out in front of me, desperate to hold my baby. I wanted to grab him and run, take him home and hide him! Of course, I couldn't. David told me he is never far away and hears when you speak to him.

David said, 'He has to go back now.' 'No, NO!' I was shaking, sobbing, hysterical!

David said he had used all his energies to get to me and he loved me and was with me always.

I stood up to applause and looks of shocked, happy glances from the audience and my mum helped me out of the building. She felt I was too shocked to continue at the event. Mum has been to many similar evenings and also spiritualist churches over the years and said she had witnessed a 'miracle'.

The next few days I couldn't stop shaking, crying and I now knew beyond all doubt that my baby, my precious beautiful boy, is safe, growing, around us all the time and I will definitely see him again. I want to thank David from the bottom of my soul and with such gratitude and praise that he made contact for me and my son.

I can honestly say that my life has been changed and I can never thank David enough. I describe David now as an Earth-bound angel, on a mission to help us understand, be aware and to comfort us.

We love and miss you so much Sam, always and forever, sunshine.

Mummy, Daddy, Annalise, your little sister, and your little brother, Ciaran
XXXXXXX

Paula Swinnerton

Chapter 15

Physical Mediumship

When you're demonstrating three, maybe four nights in a week and then do private sittings too, time soon passes. After a run of 22 nights non-stop, finally I had an evening to myself, which was wonderful. I might point out, that just because I have a night to myself doesn't mean I always spend it doing something that doesn't include the Spirit World. Oh yes, on a free evening I'll maybe go to the open circle at a local or not-so-local church, or I'll take a trip out and watch another Medium demonstrate. That could be at a church, a hall or even a hotel. Sometimes, on the other hand, I'll watch TV, sit and enjoy a meal, then meditate and relax a little. You may consider that I lead a very boring life compared to the rockers amongst you, but I wouldn't change it.

Now you might ask, 'Why, David, if you get a free night, don't you do something different other than an open circle or watch another Medium, or meditate?' Well, my answer to you would be this: I like to maintain the fun element in my Mediumship. If I just demonstrated night after night, I'm sure I'd lose that pleasure and it is so essential to good communication. By going along to a circle or a service at the Spiritualist Church, I can take part for *me* – there's no pressure to have to work, there's no pressure to have to get it right either. So, by doing this, it prevents me from being overtaken by the mundane, automated Mediumship that can unwittingly creep in if we are not careful.

I have watched so many Mediums who do this work, night after night, never taking a moment actually to attend a Spiritualist Church or, indeed, even take a service at a church. I've noticed their Mediumship is tired and bland, even though the evidence is of an excellent standard. If the Medium is bored, then the audience will be bored too. Audiences who are bored can be detrimental to the Medium and, eventually, can destroy the link with the Spirit World for the evening. So it's a spiritual life for me, in the main.

I'd arrived home early, 3-45pm and having no venues or readings that evening to attend, I decided I'd just relax. Andrea was working late that night at the shop and Barry had lots of paperwork to catch up on – so freedom went to my head. I'd been at the Purple Light, Chorley the night before and I'd brought a lovely young man through to his family. Unfortunately, life had been too much for him to bear and, at a very young age, he had ended it all by his own hand. His family had been devastated, but he had made it clear to them that he was much happier in the Afterworld now than he had been for years before in our world. He clearly stated why he had made the decision to take his own life and his family confirmed that they understood his choice. He also named other members of his family and gave me information about them. It gave them much peace, to know he was fine and well on the other side of life. Then, after they had said their "thank you" to me, I began to move to Chrissie, another one of the Chorley helpers. Unfortunately, she was receiving a message from one of the other circle members. When I say unfortunately, please don't misunderstand me; it's just I had a gentleman who was becoming very impatient as he waited for their conversation to end. I could feel and sense him building up and becoming irritated with the fact that he had to wait with me until the other lady had finished giving her message. All of a sudden, the committee member was called away urgently by her family and my link decided to step back. I'd been worried about what had happened.

In my own mind, I had convinced myself that the Spirit gentleman must have wanted to warn Chrissie about a situation. Curiosity got the better of me and, as I'd got home early, I rang my good friend June to check Chrissie was all right. June confirmed Chrissie was fine and the reasons for Chrissie having to leave weren't serious. I was relieved too as even though you always want your thoughts to be correct, you don't want them to be to the detriment of others.

As June and I began talking, she told me she was going along to a demonstration of trance and physical Mediumship that night.

The trance demonstrator, apparently, was from Stansted Hall, Essex, home of the Spiritualist National Union in the UK. June explained that the evening was in aid of a church that needed extensive repairs and her friend, Blodwyn, had some tickets left if I wanted to go along. I was welcome to meet up with June and the others and sit with them. After all my experiences of trance, I decided it would be lovely to sit and watch someone else demonstrate, so I agreed. A few minutes later, June phoned me back and our night out was confirmed. After giving me directions to the place where the demonstration would be held, excitedly, I changed out of my hairdressing attire and into my casual clothes.

The demonstration was starting at 7-30pm and everyone had to be there for 7-00. That's a little different from the clairvoyance demonstrations for a number of reasons. If you are going to a demonstration of trance and physical Mediumship, before you go in you have to remove your jewellery and mobile phones. Your property is placed in a brown envelope and sealed up. All the envelopes are then kept outside the room, with an attendant. Your envelope is returned to you at the end of the demonstration.

The reasoning behind this removal of phones and jewellery, is that the trance Medium will inevitably start to expel ectoplasm, a fine gauze film which helps to create physical phenomena. This ectoplasm can fill quite a large space. In my first book, I'd told about my visit to Paris and how I woke at 3am and the room was filled with smoky clouds, like someone had left the kettle boiling over. Well, this ectoplasm always retracts back into the Medium's body. As it does so, if the room or space where the Medium is demonstrating is not of a hygienic standard, the Medium can pick up some rather nasty stuff. On the other hand, if the Medium is disturbed by a mobile phone ringing or by someone leaving the room or being too noisy, this can also make the ectoplasm retract quickly thus causing some rather nasty internal burns. Every measure must be taken beforehand to ensure the Medium's safety, so by removing jewellery, phones, etc., you can better ensure the cleanliness and quiet that is so very necessary for this type of communication. Once you are seated, you are then told that you cannot leave the room until the end of the demonstration – no matter how desperately you may need the toilet or a cigarette; you really do have to hold on until the end.

I sat in anticipation of what I was about to witness. June chatted casually to all of us. Next, a young gentleman stood on the stage. He announced that soon the Medium would be joining us. She would be flanked by her "doorkeeper", who would be at her side if anything should go wrong and, indeed, would help when the Medium had to be brought back to physical consciousness. On the other side of her would be two others who would act as energy sources for the Medium. Again, this is quite regular and normal in this type of demonstration. We were also asked not to clap, shout or scream, or make any sudden movement towards the Medium as this could be fatal to her well-being.

Finally, we were told the house lights would go out and the stage would be illuminated solely by red lights. Red lights help the audience members to identify clearly Spirit manifestations. Once the Medium had sat down and was settled we would have a sing-song and the song would be *You are my sunshine* – its choice being typical of this type of demonstration. The singing of a song helps to lift the vibrations and atmosphere in the room, again making the Spirit's passage a lot easier.

The Medium was introduced by name and led out in silence onto the stage. The auditorium lights were then turned out and we were in pitch black. Only the stage remained lit up by the red lights. You could see the Medium begin to relax as we started to sing. Everyone joined in and it was rather uplifting just to hear people singing. I used to sing that particular song to my niece when she was a child; it certainly evokes happy memories for me and I am sure it does for others too.

As the singing reached its chorus, I began to experience the strangest of feelings. My body tingled from head to toe and my crown felt as if the hair on it was standing on end. I could feel a slight drawing sensation, almost all the front of my chest and tummy area was being pulled towards the stage area where the Medium sat in a trance state. I began to panic a little, simply because I am usually in control, or as much as any other Medium who does this work. This pulling sensation was drawing me so much I panicked lest I should slip into an involuntary trance. I tried to image a mirror in my psychic eye and reflect the feelings. In fact, I tried most techniques to stop the feelings I was experiencing but they just didn't work. The feelings intensified.

June turned round. 'You O.K., David?' she mouthed.

'Yes, I just feel a little strange, June,' I whispered back.

'Just try and relax,' she offered.

As we came to the end of the song, the sense of drawing was almost unbearable; but for the room being filled with hundreds of people and the dangers which surround the trance Medium in demonstration, I really would have left the room. Maybe it was my own sensitivity to blame, but it was the strangest feeling I had experienced, ever. At least the feelings I'd experienced in the Taxi Club at Liverpool were bearable – this was bordering on the downright painful.

I asked Jason to draw close. I could see him at the side of me. Maybe he could help, I thought to myself. 'Jason,' I asked in my head voice, 'what's happening to me? I feel terrible.'

'David, sometimes when we sit in front of a trance or physical Medium in such a situation as this, our own senses awaken involuntarily. Our own senses recognise the energies surrounding us and it just so happens, David, you are a very sensitive Medium. I will do my best to help you shut off from these energies.'

'Thanks Jason and thanks for the explanation.' It was as if a weight had been lifted from me – the sensation faded into nothing. 'Thank God for that,' I thought.

The gentleman stood up and told us that the demonstration was about to begin and, after all the Spirit guides of the trance Medium had introduced themselves to us, we could put our hands up and ask them any spiritual questions to which we wished to know the answer. Also, at the end of the demonstration, we could comment on any physical phenomena we had witnessed. Physical phenomena manifest in many different ways. Sometimes, the Spirit World places different facial features on the Medium, or at other times they will stand behind or at the side of the Medium as they are working and you can see them plainly.

The trance Medium fell deeper and deeper into her trance state. To us, the audience, it was as if she were sleeping. All of a sudden, a gentleman's voice projected forward. He told us his name and that he was a doctor. He gave some philosophy on life and how he felt our planet was changing; then he was asked a question by one of the audience members which, strangely, the doctor didn't answer. What he did say was he felt one of the other guides, who was a French lady, would be able to answer the question in much more depth and detail.

Then, the French lady came forward and did just that and it was fascinating to watch. You could see all the different characters overshadowing the Medium. Next, a Red Indian chief made himself known to us and talked about the Spirit World. As he did, a huge feather head-dress slowly began to appear around the Medium's head – the manifestation was absolutely fantastic. The head-dress appeared plainly and you could hear gasps from the audience as it did so. I looked at the people's faces close by and they all seemed completely engrossed. Then the chief asked if anyone should like to ask a question and I put my hand up and shouted, 'Yes, please.' The Indian chief replied, 'Yes friend, please ask your question.'

'I'd like to know if it is true that physical Mediumship can shorten your physical life – can it reduce the length of your life here on Earth in other words? Second, when people on Earth are chosen, by the Spirit World to be Mediums, they are given the gifts of mental or physical Mediumship, or the ability to be psychic artists. Can they then simply use that single aspect of Mediumship only or can they choose to add other skills if they feel they are able to use them?'

The chief then replied, 'I will not answer these questions as there is a guide here who wishes to answer the questions for you.'

You could see the chief start to step into the background. The trance Medium sat flopped slightly forward now. As we all stared at the Medium, a head-dress of a different kind began to appear around the Medium's head. It was obvious to me that an Egyptian youth was coming forward. As he did so, his image was as plain as day as it overshadowed the Medium.

'Hello everybody,' a young boy's voice projected from the Medium's mouth.

'Hello,' everyone called back. The boy's voice sounded like he was in his early teens, 12 or 13. 'My name's Sussie and I am Egyptian.'

Well, you could have knocked me down with a feather. That is the name of the young Egyptian lad who sometimes works with me in the Spirit World.

'Hello, sir,' Sussie shouted.

'Hi, Sussie,' I shouted back.

'Now in answer to your question, Spirits wouldn't want to work with you if it were going to harm you in any way at all. They only want to work with you if you're going to be happy and comfortable with them. The Spirit World would never do anything to endanger your life, sir,' he replied. 'I'm having fun,' Sussie said, changing the subject, 'Lots and lots of fun. I've been in your home and looked around your bedroom.'

'I know,' I replied.

'And I've been playing on your lounge floor. I have been having lots of fun.' He began to laugh loudly. June looked at me, puzzled.

'Now sir, to continue ... Mediums are given a gift. All Mediums are different so all Mediums' gifts are different, but each gift can be developed if the Medium so chooses. If you don't particularly like the way it is developing, you can ask us in the Spirit World to help you to change it and we will do that, you know, we are your friends.' Sussie gave a little giggle.

'Sir, you're on the right pathway. The Spirit World love to work with you and they watch all the good that you do on the Earth plane – they think you're great,' Sussie acknowledged.

'Thank you,' I replied.

'I think you're great too,' Sussie answered back. 'You're so much fun. I like to come and see you in your sleep, don't I?' Sussie said.

'You do keep me awake,' I joked. (But, in fact, it was the truth.)

'I do, but always know I'm there if you need me sir and, if I am being too naughty or disturbing you too much, please tell me and I'll stop.'

'O.K., I will then,' I replied.

'I am having lots of fun here but I've got to go as someone else wants to come through and speak to you all. So nice to see you, sir. 'Bye everyone, enjoy the rest of your night,' Sussie said and left.

It was so strange that the young Egyptian boy should come through another Medium and give me such wonderful proof. It was all true what he said. He had kept me awake talking and playing silly games with other Spirit children. He gave his name, which was absolutely spot-on. Well, I don't suppose you could get any better evidence than that.

At the end of the demonstration the Medium was brought back to our consciousness. She looked rather drained and tired. She'd been in trance for over an hour and I know from experience that trances can be pretty draining, if you are not careful. Tea and coffee were being served at the back of the room, so I decided that a hot drink was next on the agenda.

June came up to me. 'Did that young man and what he said make sense, love?'

'Certainly did. I couldn't believe it, June. That young Egyptian boy, Sussie, is always visiting me in my sleep state and when he said about playing in the bedroom it was all spot-on and true, June, all of that information.'

'Oh well, David love, that's great confirmation for you then, isn't it?'

'It is indeed, June.'

June began to mingle and I queued up for coffee. There were lots of familiar faces around me, all very friendly. After collecting my hot drink, I made my way over to the Medium. I wanted to ask her if she remembered anything of what had occurred throughout the demonstration and whether was she aware of it at all. Some Mediums say they are aware, some Mediums say they aren't. I usually am when I do trance demonstrations, but there have been occasions where I have been nearly detached. On one occasion, I was in a trance demonstrating and I was standing at the side of my physical body watching it as the Spirit man, who incidentally was crippled when he was to Earth, occupied it. That was, truly, a strange experience.

The Medium was very interesting; she said she had no idea of what was going on at all, which I could understand. I asked her lots of questions which she seemed only too happy to answer in full. Well, as she quite rightly pointed out, the only way to learn is to ask. As I left, a man came over to me. I recognised him as the younger man who had been on the stage. He beckoned me.

'Excuse me,' he said.

'Hi,' I said smiling.

'Can I just say, you have a wonderful gift yourself, not only of mental Mediumship but also of trance and physical Mediumship too? If you ever want to know more about it, here is my number, you would be great. Colin Fry is in our society too, he also has other wonderful gifts as well as his communication abilities.'

'Great, thanks very much,' I replied.

'Have you ever been to Stansted?' he asked.

'No, never,' I replied.

'Oh, you would love it there. What a place. It's a great atmosphere for spiritual people like you. It's full of like-minded Mediums. It's a bit like Harry Potter's school for wizards, Hogwarts,' he joked. 'You should go for a few days.'

'I'll bear it in mind, but thanks for the number and I'll certainly consider what you have said.' And with that I left. Obviously, he could tell, from the way I was talking before with the guides, that I was a Medium, but he said some nice words and, perhaps, one day I shall go to the Sir Arthur Finlay College at Stansted, Essex for a few days.

That night was another one of those nights – I was plagued; I didn't have a great night's sleep at all. I became aware of a little girl just peeking around the bedroom door smiling.

'Hello,' I said in my head voice.

'Hello cheeky,' she smiled back.

'Why are you here?' I asked.

'I am playing. You're David,' she said plainly. Now this little girl was audient. That means I could hear her clearly. Most other children that we speak to, in similar circumstances, have been sentient – they have impressed words and feelings clearly on me.

'My mummy wants to speak to you one day,' the little girl said smiling radiantly. 'She says you can help her be happy again. My mummy is sad,' the little girl continued. 'She is sad inside. She told my daddy and I listened.'

'And is mummy going to call me?' I asked the little girl.

'Yes, but she is going to watch you too.'

'O.K. then, when I see her shall I tell her you love her?' I enquired.

'Yes,' the child replied.

'And what's your name then?'

'Emma,' the child replied immediately.

'All right then Emma, I will speak to your mummy and we'll chat and you can join in too if you want to.'

'Yes please,' Emma replied. 'My mummy is Princess Patricia.'

'Well, when your mummy is close to me you come and tell me and I'll talk to her and make her smile from the inside out. Would you like that Emma?'

'Yes,' the little girl replied. At that I began to drift off. As I did, I must have opened my eyes for some reason and I still don't know what the reason was, only that when I did so, I was looking through a mist, a foggy haze and I could see little people all lined up in the fog, little children. They just stood staring at me and I can remember rubbing my eyes. I thought I was dreaming. No, this was no dream, this was real, very real and to be honest, I felt a little afraid. But my fear soon subsided as they began to wave and smile at me from the silence of the night. I could hear shouts,

'Hello, David. Hello, David.' The whole experience was amazing, such a lovely privilege. The Spirit children began to move off into the distance and the mist faded.

I just lay on my back staring into the darkness. As I did, my Egyptian guide, Sussie, stepped forward. 'Hello, David,' he said smiling.

'Hello, Sussie,' I replied.

'Well, are you happy?' he asked. What a strange question to ask in the early hours of the morning.

'Well, I am not sad,' I answered.

'All these children want your help David. They want to talk to their mums and dads. Will you help please?' he asked.

'Of course Sussie, but I need my sleep if I am to help anyone.'

'Yes, we must not disturb you any more in your sleep,' Sussie answered. 'They will be so happy that you will help them David.'

'Thank you for coming to me in the trance demonstration Sussie,' I said in my head voice. 'It was so validating, so comforting for me to know you were around me.'

Sussie smiled. 'I love to work with you David; you are so kind to all people. I was a slave boy in Egypt and I was treated very badly, but you are a kind man and I love you a lot,' he said.

'That's very nice of you to say those words, Sussie.' You know, I was actually starting to feel emotional and if I am being honest, I shed a tear or two as he spoke – it was a bit like a Lassie film, do you remember? Well, perhaps it was before your time, but Lassie was a collie dog and she pulled off the most amazing rescues you had ever seen. The dog always seemed to be able to make your emotions flow for some reason. You empathised with Lassie so much that when she made those amazing rescues you found yourself completely engrossed and upset. This was exactly how I felt when Sussie came through and spoke those kind words.

'I must leave you now to get some sleep, if you are to help my friends here in the Afterlife.' He smiled and left.

Some use actually going to sleep now, I thought, as the dawn chorus sang their familiar song outside. I must have dropped off to sleep as I had to be woken by Andrea. 'It's 8-15, David, come on we're going to be late,' she added.

I am simply no use in the mornings whatsoever. I am like a dead body, really I am. It takes one shower and five mugs of coffee to get me motivated. Then I am so hyperactive with the "caffeine kick" that there's no stopping me. But this particular morning I'd have needed dynamite in my boots to get me moving. Life's not good when you have had disturbed sleep and I am a man who needs my sleep all the time.

Clumsily, I walked downstairs. Andrea kissed me and left. 'See you in work,' she smiled. ''Bye, love.'

''Bye, Andrea.' She left. Then, grabbing a light breakfast which consisted of a banana and a biscuit, I left to follow her. As I got near the end of the lane to join the motorway, I couldn't help thinking I'd forgotten something. Then it dawned on me – I'd got all the way to the motorway and I'd forgotten my underpants and shoes. I was driving in my bedroom slippers and I had no underwear on! Oh, No! That, everybody, is how much I need my sleep. Very quickly I rang the salon and spoke to Sue. 'Going to be late love, I've forgotten a very important part of my attire.'

Sue laughed. 'Go on then, tell me what you have forgotten,' she demanded.

'My underpants ...' Sue burst out laughing. '... and my shoes, Sue!'

'Bloody hell,' she exclaimed. 'You'll have to make sure your trousers don't fall down or we'll all be in shock.'

I left Sue choking with laughter and rushed back home. You know, when I am up on that stage in front of all the people I look ever so professional. If only they knew what was going on behind the scenes. This is a bit like "confessions", isn't it? Emma and Sussie had a lot to answer for, that's for sure, but the urgency and laughter had awoken my senses.

That night I was demonstrating at Warrington – I just hoped I would be on form by then.

Warrington came round and yes, I was awake. How, I don't know, but I was there in full force bringing lots of welcome messages. I had brought through one younger man in his early 20s, who had crossed in a motorbike accident and his mum was so upset she could not even answer. We give members of the audience a microphone as the energy from their voices helps me to communicate with their loved ones. Also, I think it is better that other members of the audience can hear the responses made by the recipient of a message. It gives them confidence that they too will be able to use the all-important microphone when their turn comes for a message.

The lady began to come around a little; it was such a lovely contact. My heart bled for her son. He had gone out on his bike to get some fish and chips and, not 600 yards from his home; he was knocked off the bike by an oncoming vehicle. He was killed instantly. His mum was able to take the evidence and she understood what I meant when I said, 'You could hear police and ambulance sirens going off but you never thought it would be connected to your son.'

She just cried openly then said, 'Yes, that's true, David.'

There had been another link with a little boy too. The young man had a stillborn son whose spirit helped his mum with the link. Finally I said to her, 'What's tomorrow love, what's special about tomorrow?'

The lady answered, 'Yes, it is special.'

I just looked up and said, 'It's a funeral. Is it his?' The lady just stared in disbelief.

'Yes, it is his funeral tomorrow,' the lady added.

'Well, know your son is well in the Spirit World. He knows you're upset, but he wants you to know that tomorrow, you only lay to rest the vehicle in which he journeyed around this plane – not him. He is fine and he has never left your side. Now my dear, who is Emma?' I asked.

'My daughter,' the lady replied.

'She is here at my side.' A lovely blonde girl sat at the side of the lady who had obviously been overwhelmed by the information that had been flooding out.

'Hello Emma,' I said boldly.

'Hi David,' she called back.

'Hope you're well,' I added. 'I know you have a brother in the Spirit but I also know you have a daughter there too. Do you understand, my love?'

'Yes, yes I do David.'

'I see a sweet little girl. She comes around me now and tells me her name is Emma too. Does this make sense?'

'Yes, David, it does indeed.'

'She wants you to know she is around you always and loves you very much. She tells me you have been having a hard time with your family problems and your personal life too and she needs you to know she sees you crying very often.'

'Oh David, is she O.K.?' Emma asked.

'She's fine; she is here with your brother. She now tells me you have named a teddy after her.'

'Yes, I did. I had one of her teddies and I called it after her. I take it to bed at night and cuddle it. I know it sounds silly, but it really does give me comfort.'

'It doesn't sound silly. Anything that gives you comfort, or helps relieve your distress is only for your good. Remember, Emma will always be watching over you. Just know she and your son, both love you.'

I made this clear to Emma and her mum and they both became overwhelmed. We, who have relatively normal lives, have really got to be thankful. But to lose a son, then a granddaughter or a brother, then a daughter must be really hard. I would imagine it would make you question life strongly. Some people, who have great losses, question if there is a God. Well yes, there is a God. I've never met him, but I'm told of the force of God and the good that surrounds us all, always. Where evil, badness and negativity are, good and God are there too, helping us battle through and, in the main, to conquer their very presence. The God-force that surrounds us all is a very definite positive energy and I, for one, would not like to live my life without its presence in my world. To know God, is to know all that is good in your world. Always remember, the force of God and goodness is the most strong and dominant force in anyone's life. Never cut it out, no matter what happens in your world. Even if you suffer the loss of a child, never deny the God-force, never blame that force. A child's body is the same as any adult's body – it can be born without a fault or develop a fault, it can be subject to imperfections. Be strong, all of you who suffer this loss, know the God-force gives me and other Mediums the ability to communicate with your loved ones. Always ask God to keep your loved ones safe, particularly, your children. The Spirit World is surrounded with positivity, so for Spirit people, positive energy makes them feel strong, at home and happy with their world.

The demonstration was over at Warrington and I sat at the back of the hotel meeting my audience as they left. Finally, Emma and her mum came over.

'Thanks David, the demonstration was fantastic. You were so spot-on with what you said about my son.'

'No, I wasn't spot-on, love,' I replied. 'It was the Spirit World. Without their input I would be nothing, only David.'

'Well, whoever it was or whatever happened, you were part of it and I feel relieved and at peace.'

Emma's grandma smiled, when her daughter Emma spoke, 'I could never have expected my daughter Emma to come through. I was happy with one link, my brother, but then to receive my daughter too – well it just makes me say, miracles do happen. David, that was such a good demonstration, it has given me peace and that's why I came, thank you.'

Emma's mum, Emma and her grandmother left. I had found the mother of my night-time visitor!

So there you have it, more undoubted proof from the Spirit World that our loved ones live, surviving the physical end of our own bodies. Emma, the little girl, sang a song that night in my bedroom. As I recall it went like this ...

'Twinkle, Twinkle little Star
Emma wonders where you are
Well Emma's mum, now you know
Of the place where we all go.

Then little Emma signed off with, 'Love you ... ' and blew me a kiss.

Chapter 16

Adrian and Susan

Do you know something? Not all my sittings flow the way I would like them to. I believe, as a Medium, your messages are only as good as the Spirit persons' communicating skills allow.

I received a call from a gentleman called Adrian who was anxious to come for a sitting with me. He was guarded and didn't tell me whom he wanted to contact, which is how I prefer it. On the phone, he stressed that his situation was desperate.

The sitting soon came round and I opened my front door to Susan and Adrian. Adrian announced himself and introduced his wife to me. They followed me into the conservatory and I invited them to take a seat. As usual, I offered them some water. Adrian appeared reserved and was not at all forthcoming with any conversation. My first thought was that he was so sceptical, that he must think I can mind-read or something. Susan seemed open to the idea of communication but, surprisingly, I later learned that Adrian had only told her about this sitting the previous evening. However, as often happens with first impressions, I was quite wrong. Adrian and Susan were lovely, ordinary people who were going through the pain of losing their son, Daniel.

'I believe that neither of you has been to anything like this before.'

Susan smiled and said, 'Yes, that is correct.'

'Well, let's begin. I am joined by a younger gentleman in the Spirit World. He only looks to be in his late teens, early 20s and he has brown hair. He makes me feel he is a son to you both. So do you have a son in the Spirit World?'

'Yes,' Susan replied.

'I feel as though I have terrible pains in my head and my body feels feeble, almost as though I have a degenerative disease such as leukaemia ...'

'No, that's wrong,' Adrian interjected.

'… but I feel my organs are closing down one by one; it's almost as though I am fading away. There is a link to Preston Hospital. Your son is showing me Preston Hospital and he is being monitored there.'

'Correct,' confirmed Susan.

At this point, I was feeling very strong head pains and feeling really quite ill. I asked the young man to step back a little and to remove his symptoms from me, which he did.

'I am being given the name of Daniel. I believe that's his name.'

'Yes,' Susan said.

'Daniel is showing me a sister to Earth, so he must have a younger sister, correct? He is telling me about a tattoo that his sister has had on the base of her back. He tells me it's awful and she's mad. Indeed, you have gone mad about it also, Adrian? He keeps saying his name is Daniel.'

Adrian and Susan looked shocked and they both began to laugh.

'Our daughter, Daniel's sister, had gone out and had a tattoo of his name on her back.' Adrian shook his head, he was smiling. 'How could you have known about that?' Susan said openly.

'He is now giving me the name of Jennifer; she's close; his sister?' I queried.

'Yes,' Susan replied.

'Also Alex or Alexander and something about an unfairness at school, in a team.'

Susan and Adrian looked at each other. It was a vague look and they didn't answer.

'He tells me he has a friend in the Afterlife called Tom; he crossed not long after Daniel, in a traffic accident.'

'Yes, that's right,' Susan confirmed.

'Daniel says, "Tell Martin we're OK. Martin needs help – he is depressed."'

Susan and Adrian again looked shocked by what their son had said to them. It was evident to me that, while Susan was totally

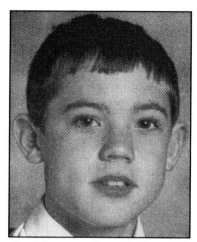

Daniel, treasured son of Adrian and Susan.

open, Adrian was still coming to terms with what I was doing.

Then disaster struck. Daniel became frustrated with the sitting and with me. He began to get agitated and said he didn't want to carry on because he couldn't do it. I spent nearly an hour coaxing him round. I felt so sorry for Adrian and Susan as things had been going great guns. I told them what was going on and Adrian said it was out of character for their son to act this way. Eventually, tactfully, I called the sitting to a close and offered to see them again. I suggested they brought their other son and daughter with them next time so that Daniel could see that his family wanted to speak to him.

Although we parted on a positive note, I wasn't happy with my sitting. And if I am not happy in my heart, I need to make myself happy. So, the next day, I rang Susan and made an arrangement to do the reading again for her and her family. It was a few weeks before this could be arranged but, as I have already stated, if I am not happy, then I have to discover why.

Susan and Adrian arrived, together with Alex and Jenny. It was my job to communicate with the missing family member and give them evidence of his survival.

'O.K. everyone, I know you are all wondering what's going to happen. I am going to connect with Daniel in the "other world" and see if he will tell me about things that I couldn't possibly know. If you understand and what I am saying is correct I need you to say 'YES, David' and, if it is wrong, then a big loud 'NO, David'. Is that all right? Anyone have any questions?'

Alex, Daniel's younger brother, looked to be bursting with questions. 'Yes, I have,' raising his hand as if he were in the class-room. 'Is he here in this room, like here, now?'

I took a look through into the Spirit World and I could see Daniel standing at the side of Jason. 'Yes, he is here.'

Jenny looked a little stunned. Alex exclaimed 'Wow, like here, now!'

'Yes Alex, here now – he's showing me a cricket bat, do you understand?'

Adrian smiled and looked at Alex. 'Well, tell him.'

Alex said, 'Yes.' He was just about to add something else, when I hushed him.

'Oh, and something has been unfair about a team or something?'

'Yes,' Alex replied.

'So you play cricket and there is a new bat?'

Alex said, 'Mmm, maybe.' He smiled.

'Now he tells me your house is for sale, with XYZ,' and he named the estate agents. It was a coincidence that I had bought my house five years earlier from the same estate agents.

Susan smiled, 'Correct.'

'He now says it's not moving at all.'

'Yes, that's right,' Susan confirmed.

'He likes your glasses, Susan; he says you bought them at trade price.'

Susan smiled again.

'He says someone related to you is an optician. Oh, it's you Adrian, you're an optician.'

'Yes I am,' Adrian added.

'He is showing me lots of boxes of glasses; he says you've gone over the top with frames.'

Susan looked at Adrian, who was smiling. 'Yes,' Susan said.

'And you have been sorting them out recently, Adrian?'

'Yes,' he replied.

'Now he tells me one member of your staff, who is Polish, has just left. You have been very busy.'

'Yes, that's right,' Susan commented.

'He is worried about his dad being stressed. "Don't overdo it, dad," he says.' They all gave Adrian a knowing look. 'Daniel says you have been contemplating purchasing or have just bought a new piece of equipment. He says you were talking to someone about it.'

'Yes,' confirmed Adrian.

'He says you would like to expand and he is showing me a row of shops and a newsagent's. Do you understand?' At this point I remember thinking if it is a newsagent's they are buying, rather them than me – the early-morning starts are a killer.

'I understand the row of shops and there is a newsagent's there, but I don't understand why he is showing you that, said a puzzled Adrian and, 'Yes, I do want to expand, or should I say that I have been considering it.'

'OK, he takes me to Leyland, a place I've never visited, but he links me to there.'

'Again I understand,' added Adrian.

'Yes,' Susan interjected, 'does he not say why he is showing you?'

I couldn't tell them a reason and as much as I asked Daniel, I was still unable to get a clear answer from him. Susan and Adrian looked a little disheartened by this – I understood what they were feeling.

'I want to talk about a birthday in March that's around my birthday on the 17th, so I would say that's the 16th or 18th.'

Susan and Adrian smiled again; the 18th was Daniel's birthday. Jenny was looking a little left out as she sat quietly listening to what was going on. In my head voice, I asked Daniel to talk to me and give evidence for Jenny as she was so quiet and I didn't want her to be overlooked. Daniel then made me aware that Jenny had just had her hair cut and coloured the weekend before and her friend had gone to the same hairdresser and copied the style. When I gave this information to Jenny she confirmed it to be right.

'Daniel now talks about Chris, who is close – either a friend or boyfriend?'

'Yes,' Jenny replied again.

'He tells me you had a shopping trip to Preston. You had birthday money to spend, £80 or so.' Jenny seemed puzzled, so Susan helped her add up the various amounts of money she had received for her birthday. Sure enough, it was correct.

'Now Daniel takes me into Staples, the stationers' shop, where you bought pens, pencils, rulers and pads for school. Is that true?'

'Yes,' agreed Jenny.

'Then you went into New Look and bought a top. That is correct isn't it, because Daniel is showing me?'

'Yes,' chorused Susan and Jenny.

'Then you were looking at boots in the shoe shop ... '

'Yes, yes,' Susan said.

'... and also you were looking at a shirt in a clothes shop and you didn't know whether to buy it for Adrian or not.'

'That's right,' Susan confirmed.

'Daniel says, "My Mum loves shopping."'

Adrian smiled and joked, 'He's not wrong there.'

Thankfully, they all laughed, which broke the ice a little as a tense feeling had come over the room. I felt Adrian's wit had dispelled this and I was glad.

'Daniel says you had lunch out. He shows me a cheese toastie and a coffee. He is smiling.'

For some reason, I felt this last piece of evidence, which was accepted, almost devalued the sitting completely and, from that moment on, I found it difficult to connect with Daniel. My evidence weakened and, in the end, I almost lost my own sense of logic. I believe it's true to say that people only remember the last bit of evidence and my last bit seemed of little consequence. Maybe I was trying too hard for this family in need or, perhaps, it was because I liked them and I was trying more than I should have.

As Susan says in her own words later, maybe it's because they want her son and that's all. But still I wasn't happy and if I'm not happy then I have got to know why. On the strength of my disappointment, I agreed to call at Susan and Adrian's house to see if I could connect a little stronger there. *My* drive, *my* need for a more successful reading was taking over and that wasn't good. In due course, I arrived at their home and was immediately made to feel comfortable. I sat in a lovely armchair and, as I did so, Daniel came forward. He told me it was his chair and it was normally positioned on the other side of the room. I ran this information past the family and received confirmation. I then described a teddy bear and asked Susan if she would she bring it to me. I held on to this bear the whole evening; I wouldn't let go. I told Susan, 'It was one that was bought for Daniel when he was in hospital.' Although Susan accepted this, she later told me that Daniel was, in fact, cross with her for buying the bear as he said he wasn't a baby and she was made to take it home. I felt Daniel was trying to over-shadow me a little and I thought I could give stronger evidence if I allowed him to do this. I then felt a little uncomfortable for a moment as I looked into the Afterworld. An older man joined Daniel. He was slightly rounder in shape, his hair had disappeared – he was quite bald. He told me he had crossed very quickly and pointed to his chest. He gave me the name of Robert/Bob. As I relayed this back to the family, Susan became emotional and the family quietened.

'My dad, it's my dad,' Susan exclaimed openly.

The children sat motionless. 'Daniel says your dad is driving him mad. He won't leave him alone. He's trying to be with his mates but your dad is there all the time.' I could sense Daniel's feelings strongly. Susan burst out laughing and everyone followed suit.

'Sounds about right, David. Doesn't it love?' she said turning to Adrian and he just smiled.

'Daniel tells me you've had problems with the garage roof and his vehicle is in the garage too.'

'Yes, it is,' Adrian confirmed.

'He takes me to the middle of your garden – I feel like I'm digging up the middle of the lawn. Do you understand?'

'No'. Susan was puzzled. 'No, I can't say that means anything.' However, Adrian spoke up with a definite 'Yes'. Susan still looked confused.

'Yes, the pond. I got him to dig the pond out just before he took ill, remember?' Then it clicked with Susan.

'He says, "Don't feel guilty about that."' Adrian looked emotional; obviously, Daniel's words had touched a nerve.

'Well I did; he was ill and I had asked him to clean the pond out.'

'Yes, but you didn't know he was ill,' Susan exclaimed.

'I can't help feeling responsible though,' stated Adrian.

I then began to see a cemetery. 'Daniel is showing me the cemetery where his body is. He says it's nearby and he is buried next to his grandad, near the wall on the far side, just up the road.'

Susan spoke and confirmed this; then silence fell on the room. For some reason I again began to struggle with my Mediumship. Daniel was trying to get me to identify a statue and some football memorabilia. He had his mum and me hunting all over the house. I believe that my Bridge to Angels had gone a bridge too far. Again, I became taxed by the communication and the sitting ended once more on a negative note. Strangely, I couldn't understand why. Why was this happening to me again? I wasn't happy and again I asked to re-sit Susan and Adrian.

I am like a dog with a bone, Andrea says. My final sitting came round and the family arrived at our house. Smiling and in good spirits, Daniel came bouncing through and told me that at one time his parents had been out around Southport looking at houses. They had seen a big old terraced house and were considering renovating it. They had driven for hours around the neighbourhood and he directed me to the back of the Scarisbrick New Road area. Daniel told me his dad had also considered buying a shop and house combined again. All of this Adrian and Susan accepted.

Daniel then mentioned an accident involving someone's foot and again it was accepted as correct. He then mentioned that his mother, Susan, had called for a couple of sandwiches from a take-away. Adrian had eaten his but Susan did not eat hers, saying it was awful. As he recounted all of this, he told me he had been with them, sitting in the back of their car.

Susan was amazed but Adrian said, 'Why should he say these trivial things when there is far more important stuff to talk about?' Susan looked at him, 'But come on Adrian, how could David have known that and the accident with your foot in the supermarket? How?'

Adrian turned to me. 'It's not that I don't believe you David, but why does he talk about this when he could talk about so much more important matters?'

I could only give my answer as I saw it. 'Maybe he is telling you in his own way that he is watching you. As Mediums, we can only give what we are given. It is not us. He says Jenny has had chest complaints and was in hospital.' Susan confirmed this. 'No more flowers, mum,' he has added.

Susan hit the nail on the head when she then remarked, 'Maybe we just want you to give us our son back, David. Maybe we are expecting too much.'

As I was writing this piece on Susan and Adrian and their family, I'd tried to ring their home to query some evidence but could get no answer. I continued to write and as I did so, the telephone rang and it was Adrian. He explained the phone at home was playing up and the call was diverted to his mobile. I didn't have the heart to say it was him I was writing about at the time. I told him I just wanted to ask Susan something and he volunteered to call her and ask her to ring me back. When she did so, my query was about the evidence of Bob, her father. As I began to reel it off to her, she interrupted me and said, 'It's my dad's anniversary today, David.' I wished the floor could have swallowed me up. 'I can't apologise enough Susan,' I replied. I felt awful, just awful, but Susan told me not to worry.

After putting the phone down from her, I thought back to the beginning of my journey, my spiritual journey and how far I'd come. It had been a long, hard slog but one that to this day I do not regret. I've had the privilege of meeting lovely people, just like Susan and Adrian and their children. It is with all their love that I am able to carry on forward and continue to be the Bridge to your Angels.

Dear David,

I have found this quite difficult (maybe Daniel finds the same!). I really want to believe there is more and odd facts do seem to point to this. However, there seem to be such important facts that he hasn't mentioned that I am still finding it very difficult to understand.
I have read your book and know all the facts enclosed are true. I know you are a genuine person and wish only to help others. I wonder if it is simply my greed that I am not satisfied, because whatever we gain from you will never replace Daniel for us.

Susan Halsall

Chapter 17

Danielle

Time is tight for me at the present. I'm even finding it hard to keep on working in my hairdressing salons. It's really strange – when I first set out on my spiritual journey and went public, I really thought my family, friends and customers would not support me, but just the opposite has happened. Since then, just four years ago, the tremendous support from the public and my family and friends has spurred me on. My only sadness in all of this is that I can't help everyone. One family had been on my list for over three years, so the plight of people's grief must be addressed. No matter what some organisations say, whether they be religious or otherwise, there is a definite place for Mediumship in our society today.

One Monday evening, Brian rang me to say our website "techies" had telephoned to alert him to an email that had just come in which concerned them greatly. It was from a lady called Barbara Watson. He told me she had explained in the message how she was desperate to speak to me, as her grief and loss were taking over her and her husband's life. Brian was not given any details other than that her life was being consumed by grief. A phone number was provided in case I could do anything for them. As Brian spoke to me, I was on my way to Lancaster to give a demonstration and he asked if I would take the number. I agreed, but said I would have to pull off the motorway first. I told him there were no promises, none, that my one-to-ones were taking over and soon it would be pointless sleeping. Brian laughed loudly and then read her number to me. I said my goodbyes and continued on my journey. As I was driving, my guides were talking to me. I just knew Barbara was desperate and the sense of her desperation almost enveloped me. I felt very sad for her. In the background of my vision, I could see a young man, very smart, with brown hair and he just sat looking at me. Then he said quite strongly, 'Please will you call our Barbara. I need you to call her.' I was a little taken aback with his absolute strength to come right out and say what he wanted of me. I agreed I would call her after the demonstration and I asked him to step back. This he did almost immediately. As I've said in an earlier part of the book, talking to Spirit and driving don't mix; just like liquid spirit – it affects your concentration when driving.

The demonstration at Lancaster went well – in fact, it was completely sold out. The hall was full to bursting and people seemed to be happy. At the end, I was inundated with requests to sign books or to attend and demonstrate at other venues. I was even invited to Canada, but declined, of course, due to the number of one-to-one sittings I have to satisfy. Time had passed quickly and with another demonstration successfully over with, I began my journey home. As I headed across the Lancastrian countryside, I began to see that my friend, the young dark-haired man was back. 'Just reminding you,' he urged. 'Barbara, call Barbara, please!' he pushed. I replied, 'O.K.' and with Barbara's number already in my phone, I gave her a call. It was engaged. The young man looked disappointed.

Danielle, the shy daughter of Peter and Barbara Watson.

'Don't worry, I'll try again,' I said. I called again but it was still engaged. For 20 minutes I tried and each time it was engaged. I looked towards where the young man had been but he was no longer there. 'Oh well,' I thought, 'he must have become tired of waiting.' Not likely! Two seconds later he was back.

'I thought you had gone,' I said out loud.

'No, Barbara's on the phone to her friend. Try again

soon.' As I drove nearer to home, I tried the number again and, this time, it rang. Barbara answered.

'Hi,' I said, 'I'm David Traynor.' Barbara seemed full of surprise but I could tell she was overjoyed that I'd actually called her; overjoyed and relieved, I suspect. As Barbara began to speak, I apologised for interrupting her and I explained that before she started to give me her information, it was important that she didn't include anything about her sadness, as it was my job to tell her. She seemed puzzled when I said this but I think she realised why I did.

'Barbara, as I speak to you over the phone I am made aware that there is a young man in the Afterworld. Very smart, only early 30s. Can you understand someone of that age, Barbara?'

'Yes,' she acknowledged.

'Now he talks to me about his head, so he had problems around his head which took him over to the Afterworld, would that be correct?'

'Yes.'

'Who is Andrew?'

'That's him, my brother.'

'Great, now I feel there is someone else you are desperate to hear from but it's a little difficult now over the phone. You understand, don't you?'

'Yes, yes I do.'

'Andrew tells me you have been really heartbroken. He needs you to know he is close to you and wants you to know he loves you very much.'

'Thanks, David.'

'He seems quite a clever young man.'

'I don't know, I wouldn't say clever,' Barbara teased.

'Well, maybe I misunderstood, Barbara. He wants you to know he is well and he'll come forward again. You're still very desperate, aren't you?'

'Yes, David, I am. I believe in what you do, I've had signs. I lie in bed at night willing my loved one to come forward and touch me. I get a strange tickling feeling on my crown. I know it's them trying to give me a sign. I'm right, aren't I David?' Barbara asked.

'Yes, you are. Does it give you comfort, Barbara?'

'Yes, it does. I, well we, my husband and I, live from day to day.'

'Well, I will see you soon. I have a slot, it's a cancellation. I don't get many but I'll let you have it and we will see if your loved one will come forward and let you know all about him or her. How does that sound?'

'Great,' Barbara replied, 'I'm desperate.'

With that I bade her good-night. Two days later, a text message appeared on my mobile phone from Barbara asking why I hadn't called her back with the appointment. Sometimes, it's difficult to return the call immediately because of the volume of requests I receive daily. So I sent a text to her saying that I hadn't forgotten and I would text again in the coming days with a slot. I received a reply apologising for her mithering – a good northern word meaning "pestering". On the contrary, I replied, she hadn't – she was just acting out of desperation, something that I understand and relate to completely.

After I came away from my mobile phone, a lovely-looking, young girl stood in my sight line. She was definitely in the Afterworld. She had long, light brown hair, trimmed round her face. She was slim and very attractive and she looked to be aged about 16 or 17. I said "Hello" to her but she didn't react. She just stood still, staring at me. I said "Hello" again but still she said nothing. She stayed with me for a short while, then left. In fact, as quietly as she had appeared, she disappeared. I thought no more of it.

Some days later, I rang Barbara to fix the appointment and, as I did so, the young lady appeared again, only this time she smiled a little and said the word "mum". 'Is Barbara your mum,' I asked, but the girl stayed silent and still, like a picture. I had a strong sense that this girl was Barbara's daughter in the Afterworld, but I couldn't be sure enough to call Barbara back because the young lady didn't want to speak to me. So I decided it was best to wait until Barbara and her husband came for their sitting – maybe then I would get a clearer understanding of who she was. Monday soon came around and the front door bell rang. As I opened the door, I was confronted by a small, dark-haired lady and a very tall, well-built gentleman. As I looked at Barbara, I immediately knew the girl was her daughter – she was the image of her. A bright "Hello" came from Barbara, but her husband didn't seem quite so comfortable. 'Hi, welcome,' I replied, showing them into my home.

I must point out they were both concealing their grief well but their devastation was so deep, it was hard for me to leave them alone in my conservatory whilst I went to bring some water. They were like two lost souls, lost in a sea of life that really they didn't want to be a part of. I thought to myself, 'Stuff the water, cut to the chase and return to the conservatory.'

'Now there is a young lady and I know she is definitely with you. She is here in the Afterworld and she looks like you Barbara. Have a seat.' They both stood staring at me. 'Have a seat,' I prompted a second time.

'Thank you,' said Barbara.

'This young lady, she is your daughter. She is in the Spirit.'

'Yes,' they replied in unison.

Just as the word "Yes" left their lips their real sadness and grief began to emerge. 'I believe your daughter is telling me things were not right about her passing – she keeps giving me feelings that something, some situation about her crossing, was not quite right. She now says, "It's not fair."'

Barbara and her husband looked puzzled, yet they said nothing.

'She's just said the words "her head is mashed" and she needs you to know she was having problems with PE at school. She didn't want to get changed for PE and she played truant.'

Barbara looked at her husband then turned to me and quite definitely said, 'No, she didn't play truant.'

Barbara's daughter was clearly saying, 'I did, yes I did.' 'She is showing me she registered for the lesson, but having decided she wasn't doing it, she walked past the changing rooms,. She then gives a sense of relief that she got out of it. It's really clear to me – are you sure you don't understand this?' I asked again.

'Well, yes, she did have a big problem one day with the PE teacher.'

'Yes, she is saying "yes" to me,' I replied.

I turned round at that point because Barbara's daughter had drawn a little closer to me. She was now standing behind me at my conservatory door; she had previously been a little distant and a little nervous. Maybe this was because she was trying to understand why I could see her clearly in the Afterworld. As I turned around, a blast of a voice shouted and seemed to vibrate the atmosphere.

'Don't look at me, please don't look at me.'

'But why can't I look?' I said out loud. Barbara looked puzzled.

'Your daughter is telling me I can't look at her, Barbara, she says she is shy. She isn't very confident about herself or this situation.'

'Well, I'll try not to look at you,' I told her, 'but can you come a little closer please, your mum and dad are desperate to hear from you.'

A voice echoed back from the Afterworld, 'I am frightened, I'm frightened of you.'

'Why? I'm just David,' I replied. I looked at her mother and father. She said she was frightened of me; she made me cover the side of my face so I couldn't glance behind me. She then insisted I use both hands. Not wanting to lose my connection, I did as I was asked. I stood with both hands either side of my head – like blinkers on a horse.

Barbara looked at her husband; he looked back at me. 'That's my daughter,' he said. Barbara smiled, 'She was like that sometimes, David. She could be so lacking in confidence.'

'She is telling me her inert body had been shaken vigorously in an attempt to wake her up, then there was a feeling of pressing down on her chest, as though someone was trying to bring her back to life. Now she is showing me a syringe; that would be used to treat conditions such as diabetes for example. Yes, was she a diabetic?' I asked.

'Yes, she was,' Barbara replied. At this point I could see the shock on Pete's face.

'How would you know that?' he questioned out loud. It was as if he had been thinking those words and his thought had uncontrollably slipped out, 'How?'

Barbara gave him a little smile as she squeezed his hand. 'I told you Pete, it is true; there is an Afterworld.' Then, looking at me she said, 'He wouldn't believe it when I said ... would you?' She turned to look at her husband. Pete just stared at me. All of a sudden the years of believing, or having been brought up to believe, that death was something totally different, seemed to pale into insignificance. What he was listening to took over completely.

'She is saying she was a diabetic, she is saying, "sorry mum, sorry dad" almost as if she did this deliberately or, it is believed that it was done deliberately. Do you understand? I believe it wasn't done deliberately. I know it wasn't,' I continued.

Barbara looked emotional. 'No, it definitely wasn't, but people around our town believed it was and there had been lots of rumours. Actually, we don't yet know how she died, David – maybe this is why we are so messed up; we just don't know.'

I could sense the sadness welling up in these people. Goodness, I felt so sorry for them. If God could have taken me instead, there and then and given them back their daughter, I'd have let him – it was so overwhelming, it really was. 'Look, let me see what your daughter says about her crossing, O.K?' They nodded. Pete also seemed a little emotional at this suggestion.

'Hello, love, can you tell us how you crossed, please?'

'No I can't,' the voice of the daughter replied.

'Why can't you?' I questioned.

'Because I'm a silly fool.'

'She is telling me, Barbara, she is a silly fool – she should have listened. 'It's not your fault, mum,' she has just said to me clearly. She says she's sad. She loves you both, you're her lovely mum and dad and she wants to be here with you. She tells me, Barbara, you had gone on and on at her about diabetes and she wouldn't listen. She's saying she is sorry and showing me a diabetes meter, the kind they use for testing blood sugars. Now she shows me a syringe and then the meter again. I feel so meek, Barbara.' A feeling of weakness came over me strongly. 'So meek and weak.'

Barbara and Pete just hung on my every word. 'My guides tell me that diabetes is on your side of the family Barbara, that all your family are diabetics. It's not on your side at all Pete,' I pointed out. 'That's right,' Barbara admitted. 'Her meter was on the bedroom floor,' she added quietly.

'She now says she was having trouble at school with a couple of girls who were picking on her and even bullying her. She is laughing – she says she will haunt them.'

Barbara confirmed her daughter was having problems of that nature with two girls. Barbara laughed, 'she'll haunt them will she?'

'I haven't got your name yet.' I turned around to look at her. 'Don't look, please,' she shouted.

'O.K., O.K., sorry,' I said in my head voice. Speaking out aloud I said, 'I need your name.' 'Barbara, she looks 16 or 17.'

'Well, she died on the day before her 13th birthday but she did look much older, didn't she, Pete?'

'Yes, she did,' Pete acknowledged.

'From what I've seen of her, she does look older. Her hair is long, light brown, parted on the side and coming down round her face like this.' I gestured with my hands to emphasise how her hair hung. 'She stands about this tall.' I raised my hand to indicate her height. She seems particular with how she looks. Correct, Barbara?'

'That's my daughter.'

'She has just said something to me about Stephie. Who is Stephie?'

'Her school friend,' Barbara replied.

'She also tells me she had friends called Beth, Louise and Sarah.'

'Yes, those were her friends too.'

'Great, but she still hasn't said her name yet,' I replied. 'Now your daughter is telling me Abi was a close friend, someone she could talk to, someone she could trust and confide in. She says

Michelle is a friend of you and Pete. Michelle's relationship with you two is like Abi's with her – that of a trustworthy, close friend. She is making a comparison, you see. There is also a Rebecca, who was like a big sister to your daughter; she looked out for her when she was in the physical world.

And there is Rachael and a Julie – all close around you.'

'Yes, all these names and situations are correct ... including the statements about Rebecca.'

Pete and Barbara's daughter was trying to image me a young boy. I tried to talk her into letting me look at her but she just wouldn't. So I still had to conduct her communication with my back to her. I could still sense what she was saying. 'Your daughter tells me there is a little boy around you about this high. I was holding up my hand again. 'About four years old. He is your son.'

'Yes,' Pete replied. His reply was so anxious it was almost as if he was expecting me to say something bad was going to happen to him.

'I am getting the name of James, Jim, no James. Mmm – I am not quite getting the name correctly.'

'It is similar,' Barbara interjected.

'Jamie, that's it, Jamie ... and Danielle.' Pete nearly fell off the chair with shock. Barbara remained calm.

'Yes, that's my son's name, Jamie – and Danielle *is* my daughter's name.'

'Thanks, Danielle,' I said trying not to turn round. It felt like that game we used to play when we were kids, where you had to make the person opposite say "yes" or "no". It is sometimes impossible, isn't it?

'Oh, she says the name Kelly too.'

Barbara replied, 'Oh yes, her cousin.'

'Yes, and Helen, she says the name Helen.'

'Yes, my sister, Kelly's mum,' Pete replied looking relieved.

'And Christy, no Chrissie, no it's a "K" name. Never mind, I can't get that.' I was beginning to feel drained, to be truthful. The need to give absolute proof and evidence had overtaken me and the session was becoming a little tiring.

'Do you mean Kirsty?' Barbara asked.

'Yes that's it, and Sharon.'

'That's my sister, Danielle's aunt,' Barbara confirmed.

'Danielle is so quiet and lacking confidence, I really don't know why,' I puzzled. Maybe she thought I'm not a nice man or maybe she was very wary of strangers when she was in the physical world. 'How long is it since she passed over please?' I asked. To be honest, I was so drained now I needed to end the sitting but I wanted to do it carefully and not upset Pete and Barbara, or, indeed, Danielle.

'Six months,' Pete replied.

I couldn't believe the excellence of her communication skills after only six months in the Afterworld. She had certainly been an outstanding link. I said to Barbara and Pete, 'Please remember each time you see a Medium, she will be stronger and stronger. She needs to overcome her shyness – you may even get some physical evidence – but the shyness has to be dealt with first.'

I told Danielle I would have to stop and she understood, but Barbara seemed dismayed. I really believe her parents would have stayed in my conservatory for the rest of their lives, if I had let them, just listening and enjoying the evidence, but, as in all aspects of life, everything must end. Pete and Barbara thanked me and left.

Barbara takes up the story at this point. I believe that Pete and Barbara are two very special people, so fully committed to their family that, even after the sad loss of their daughter, they were not prepared to lose contact. Their love stretched from the boundaries of this life and into the life after. I really do believe, in my heart, that Barbara and Peter will never lose contact with their daughter. She will always be there at their sides, giving them signs, telling them how much she loves them and how much she is still a part of their lives here in the physical world.

Danielle

My name is Barbara and I have been happily married to Pete since 1987 after being together for six years. We both became proud parents of Danielle who was born on 19 May, 1994 weighing 6 lb. 14 oz. From the minute our little girl was born, our lives were changed forever. She was what we had dreamed of for years, having had several miscarriages and being diagnosed with unexplained infertility. We were both 31 years old when she came into this world.

She was welcomed by a very large family, indeed. I am the eldest of six children and Pete is also one of six. My dad was one of 14 and my mum was one of five so there were lots of aunties, uncles and cousins. Pete was running his own business, we owned our own home, had our Boxer dog and a cat – so our baby completed our little family just perfectly.

Danielle joined a ballet class just before she was four years old and took part in several shows, gaining medals and certificates along the way. She also enjoyed tap dancing. The dance teacher used to tell me that she was a credit to us and other parents spoke of how polite she was.

Danielle was diagnosed with Type 1 Diabetes when she was seven years old; a condition that is hereditary in our family. She was treated with insulin injections and between us we counted carbohydrates to work out how much insulin was needed to keep her blood sugar as stable as possible. One year later, we bought her an insulin pump which gave her freedom from injections but, after five years of being on the pump, Danielle decided she was fed up with being attached to it and wanted to be like her other school friends, who were treating their diabetes with injections and so we converted back in January, 2007.

Animals, old people and babies were what touched Danielle's heart in a really big way. She said she was going to work with sick animals, the elderly, or children when she left school. She also thought about becoming a beautician, so we even talked about buying her a little salon and helping her to run it. We couldn't ever bear the thought of Danielle leaving home one day, so we bought a house big enough to accommodate her and her own little family if she was to have one (wishful thinking). We thought about buying the house next door to us so that we could be near her if she didn't fancy living in the same house as us. This might seem too hasty, but when you have looked after a child with an illness, you can't imagine handing over their healthcare to someone else – in case something goes wrong. Not only that, we loved her too much to let her go.

Unfortunately, Danielle became a victim of bullying during her second year at high school but she managed to keep a brave face until one day when she asked me if I could help her face school. She was very tall (5' 7½") and extremely stunning and the older girls saw her as a threat so she was called names such as 'whore' and 'slag' and much, much worse. I could not send her to school for the last week of her life because I worried too much that things would get out of hand and the next stage might be that she got attacked. Instead, I made plans to have her home-educated or change schools.

Our beautiful daughter, Danielle died suddenly on 18 May, 2007, aged 12 years and 364 days. Yes, she was looking forward to her 13th birthday party the following day. She was our only daughter. She was much-loved and so protected.

On the morning of Friday 18 May, 2007 I was lying awake in bed planning the day ahead. Danielle's little brother was still asleep and I was taking advantage of the peace and quiet. I decided at 9-15 that it was about time we got moving, as we were going to the butcher for the home-made sausages and burgers and then on to the supermarket to get the birthday cake that Danielle had chosen. Friends from school and a good friend from Scotland were all coming to the party and just couldn't wait. I had always made the birthday parties extra special. This year was a Makeover Party, which was to start at 12-30pm and end whenever it ended. The girls were to arrive with no make-up (this was quite funny because they were quite embarrassed about arriving with bare faces), have their eyebrows shaped, make-up applied and nails done. There would be good music and a barbecue. However, Danielle said that it would be a waste of time having all their makeovers, if nobody could see them. So I agreed to let them all walk down to the town for a while and then come back home for some food and music.

I had taken Danielle shopping, on Thursday 17 May, for her outfit and she gave me and my next-door neighbour, Jackie, a fashion parade. I have to say, the outfit was stunning and the jewellery she had chosen was perfect. She wanted to keep the clothes on but defiantly took them off and hung them up quite neatly ready for the big day.

Getting back to that Friday morning, at 9-15, I checked on our four-year-old and was so glad to see him in a deep sleep; yet more peace, while Danielle and I had our breakfast and chatted about the day, I thought. I walked into Danielle's room and that's where the nightmare began. I turned her over and just thought she was in a deep sleep so I tried to wake her up but I knew things weren't right. I opened one of her eyes and it was still. I panicked, rang the ambulance and listened to their instructions on what to do. She wasn't breathing. I performed heart massage until extra help arrived. I thought to myself that the paramedics would know what to do and then I would soon be cuddling her to make her feel better. I was so wrong. The ambulance crew announced that she was dead as soon as they saw her. Of course, I didn't accept it and I can only describe it as a living hell. Nothing on this Earth could be any worse.

The living hell soon turned into a living nightmare, as people in the town started gossiping. It was said, even in front of me, that this poor girl was bullied at school and took her own life. I knew they were talking about my daughter but I couldn't find the strength to put them right. We kept the funeral arrangements quiet so that we didn't have any spectators looking for even more town gossip. Danielle loved horses so we made sure she had the best. Two black horses wearing plumes and velvet drapes pulled her glass carriage

*along to the crematorium and five black limousines carried her
close family behind.*

*As this was a sudden death, you can imagine what followed when
I rang the ambulance service. I had no idea what I was about to
endure. Before I knew it, my house was literally swarming with
police, crime scene investigators, ambulance crew, a doctor, then
one by one or two by two, my family started arriving with Pete's
family and then Pete was brought home by police car. It was 'not
happening' if you know what I mean. It was like I was part of a
sad movie that was taking place in my house. The officers and
investigators were like they were the film crew but deep down I was
in shock. I knew it was really happening but I didn't know what to
do. Pete asked if he could go and see Danielle but the police were
at the bottom of the stairs and another officer told him that he
couldn't see her. The doctor said that he thought he should. After
a while, the police officer said that he could see Danielle as long
as he didn't touch her. Pete said he was going to give her a kiss
but the officer said he wasn't allowed. Later on, Pete told me that
he had touched her and kissed her too. Why not? He was her
father after all. Furthermore, I had had my hands on her giving
her heart massage so why couldn't Pete touch her? It all seemed
so silly. Then it sank in! The questions we were asked made me
think that we were suspects, even though they kept on telling us it
was routine. Why were there so many officers and plain-clothes
people in my home? Why were they taking photos of some of the
rooms with those cameras? It was far too much for me to take in.
I had not even accepted my daughter had died yet and all this was
going on. When I had to hand over all her medication to the crime
scene investigators and watch them leaving the house with plastic
bags, I just couldn't stop being sick, retching with nothing there
because there was no food in my stomach.*

*Some days later, my sister and sister-in-law came to sit with me
and Pete, while the Coroner's Officer read out the post-mortem
results. They concluded that the cause of death was DIB (Dead in
Bed Syndrome) caused by diabetes but I questioned the findings*

and wanted to know the correlation of the spinal fluid glucose with a blood sample taken from her finger. This was because the glucose reading was not low enough for Danielle to have had a fit or slip into a coma. The pathologist then questioned herself and, to be absolutely certain, she sent a small sample of Danielle's heart tissue to a specialist hospital in London. Whilst waiting for these results to come back, I got myself involved in a charity called SADS UK which raises awareness of sudden cardiac death due to an underlying heart condition. I convinced myself that Danielle must have died of this or else how could I, her mum, who was responsible for looking after her and her health, ever come to terms with the fact that my daughter had died of something I could have prevented. After all, I had managed to bring her round in the past – so why not this time? The doctor told me that this only happens to diabetics once in every 15 or 20 years or one person in every 400,000 with diabetes, so there was no way this was going to be what killed Danielle; she couldn't be that unlucky, I thought.

It is nearly six months since that terrible day. On 12 November, 2007 at 6pm I went to visit David Traynor with my husband, Pete. David went on to talk to us about Danielle and explained that she was very quiet and not coming forward enough for some reason. He asked how long ago it was that she had passed over and when we explained it wasn't quite six months, he told us that if that was the case, her communication was excellent and he wouldn't normally have expected that much. He said that over the next six months she will become stronger and she may even materialise in front of us. That is if she overcomes her shyness.

David explained that Danielle could see us and knew that we couldn't see her but then realised that David could see her, which surprised her, and that is why she kept on telling him not to look. This, we believed to be because Danielle said that a lot especially when I used to stare at her in admiration.

The following morning after seeing David, I telephoned the Coroner's Office and left a message to say that I would like to accept the findings of the pathologist who did the post-mortem. I *received a phone call from the Coroner himself, who read a report that had come from the specialist in London regarding the tests carried out on Danielle's heart. They had found nothing significant and suggested that the original findings be used as the cause of death. We were going now to have to accept that diabetes was the cause of our daughter's death.*

Meeting David has changed our lives for the better. We will grieve for Danielle for a long time and will never get over losing her. However, we are convinced that there is another life that definitely exists and that it is not too far away from where we are standing. After all, how could David have known that Danielle died as a result of her diabetes when it hadn't even been declared officially as the cause of her death? Not only is David a gifted Medium, he has a wonderful, caring nature about him. Thank you, David.

Barbara Watson.

Epilogue

I cannot explain to anyone why I have been allotted the gift of being able to speak to Spirit People in the Afterlife. All I can affirm is that the Spirit side of Life does exist. It is very real and yet very difficult to understand in its entirety – and, for this reason only, I can understand people's reactions as to who I am and what I do. I truly believe with all my heart that there are many pathways that lead to the God force that surrounds us all here on Earth. It is my belief that if you lose a loved one, life has a natural way of helping you deal with your grief and loss. An alternative to the natural way is to consult a Spirit Medium who can put you in touch with your departed loved one and, through that contact, bring to you the solace and comfort of knowing that they still live on – all be it in another world. Although you can't see them or hear them they can communicate with you through a Medium.

To all parents who have loved and lost a child, never give up hope that you will hear from them again; be strong and know they are only a second away.

I leave you with a message which was placed on my website guest book by a gentleman called Glyn. He and his wife sought communication and, without any expectations, they came to see me. Here is his message:

Hello, David,

The concept of a spirit world is very new to me and difficult to comprehend on this helter-skelter earth plane but, following the devastating loss of my daughter in November, 2006 off I went trying every way I could to find her. I visited a few mediums who tried but did not really deliver in terms of accuracy or comment; I felt a little disappointed.

A friend mentioned yourself and their own special and moving experience so I decided this was a real chance to get close to my daughter in search of that one last time. There were many questions and heartaches to attempt to resolve.

I found your reading by far the best and most accurate with names that rang true, especially one of my daughter's friends who has an unusual Christian name! The messages were distinctively phrased just as we remember when she was with us. The statements also rang true regarding events and how they unfolded.

I am impressed by your ability and concern to help people who are searching for the truth. I am understanding more as time passes; that we do not die, we simply cross over onto our next journey alongside those loved ones who have gone before. What a wonderful thought that the love we have will never die.

Thank you, David; I am glad we met. God bless.
Glyn.

May I thank you all who have contributed to this book? I hope all of you who have read it understand that there is always a way to keep in touch with your loved ones in the Afterlife.

David Traynor.

Into the Light

David Traynor will be preparing his third book which will be entitled *Into The Light* and relates to true experiences of our loved ones making their transition from here on the Earth plane into the Light of the Spirit World. With this extraordinary story, David hopes to put at rest the minds of loved ones left behind and remove fears of the other side. It is hoped this will give confirmation of the place where we all go and as is promised by most of the world's religions.

David Traynor will point your way *Into the Light*.

í

ISBN 978900734417

www.davidtraynor.com

JADE PUBLISHING LIMITED